Stitch by Stitch

Volume 19

TORSTAR BOOKS

NEW YORK · TORONTO

Stitch by Stitch

TORSTAR BOOKS INC.
41 MADISON AVENUE
SUITE 2900
NEW YORK, NY 10010

Knitting and crochet abbreviations

approx = approximately	in = inch(es)	sl st = slip stitch
beg = begin(ning)	inc = increas(e)(ing)	sp = space(s)
ch = chain(s)	K = knit	st(s) = stitch(es)
cm = centimeter(s)	oz = ounce(s)	tbl = through back of
cont = continue(ing)	P = purl	loop(s)
dc = double crochet	patt = pattern	tog = together
dec = decreas(e)(ing)	psso = pass slipped	tr = triple crochet
dtr = double triple	stitch over	WS = wrong side
foll = follow(ing)	rem = remain(ing)	wyib = with yarn in
g = gram(s)	rep = repeat	back
grp = group(s)	RS = right side	wyif = with yarn in front
hdc = half double	sc = single crochet	yd = yard(s)
crochet	sl = slip	yo = yarn over

A guide to the pattern sizes

		10	12	14	16	18	20
Bust	in	32½	34	36	38	40	42
	cm	83	87	92	97	102	107
Waist	in	25	26½	28	30	32	34
	cm	64	67	71	76	81	87
Hips	in	34½	36	38	40	42	44
	cm	88	92	97	102	107	112

Torstar Books also offers a range of acrylic book stands, designed to keep instructional books such as *Stitch by Stitch* open, flat and upright while leaving the hands free for practical work.

For information write to Torstar Books Inc., 41 Madison Avenue, Suite 2900, New York, NY 10010.

Library of Congress Cataloging in Publication Data
Main entry under title:

Stitch by stitch.

Includes index.
1. Needlework. I. Torstar Books (Firm)
TT705.S74 1984   746.4   84-111
ISBN 0-920269-00-1 (set)

9876543

© Marshall Cavendish Limited 1985

Printed in Belgium

ISBN 0-920269-19-2 (Volume 19)

Step-by-Step Crochet Course

Step-by-Step Knitting Course

Contents

Crochet / COURSE 84

*Crochet scallops
*Single scallop pattern
*Scallop fabric
*Single scallop edging
*Stitch Wise: daffodil and poppy motifs
*Patterns for towel edgings

Crochet scallops

Many lace patterns, both edgings and fabrics, incorporate scallop motifs into the design. If you try a lace pattern, you may find that it is quite easy to work out how to make an isolated scallop without its surrounding motifs. These single scallops can be used as edging or repeated one on top of another to form a fabric. This course gives instructions for working a single scallop shape and illustrates how the shape can be transformed into a fabric or edging. Two-color or multi-colored scallop fabrics can also be very attractive. (See opposite page.)

Single scallop pattern

The instructions given here are for a single scallop. The size of the scallop depends on the weight of yarn and size of hook used. You will need to experiment until you achieve the size you want. You can also make the scallop smaller by stopping after the third or fourth row.

1 Make 13 chains and then begin the first row (WS) with 1 double into the 9th chain from the hook. Work 4 chains and 1 single crochet into the last chain.

2 Turn the work and begin the 2nd row with 3 chains. Work 9 doubles into the first loop, 1 double into the double, 9 doubles into the 2nd loop and 1 double into the 5th of the 8 chains.

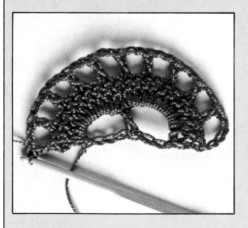

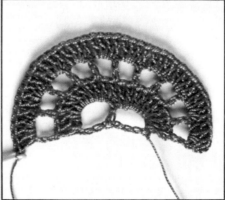

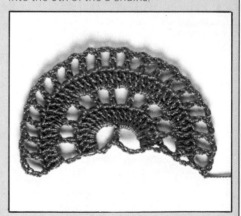

3 Turn the work and begin the 3rd row with 5 chains and 1 double into the 3rd double. Work 2 chains, skip 1 double and work 1 double into the next double all across the row, finishing with 2 chains and 1 double into the turning chain. 10 spaces formed.

4 Turn the work and begin the 4th row with 3 chains. Work 3 doubles into each 2-chain space and 1 double into each double across the row, finishing with 3 doubles into loop formed by turning chains, and 1 double into 3rd of the 5 turning chains.

5 Turn and work the 5th row in the same way as the 3rd row. 20 spaces formed. This completes one scallop. If you are going to make a scallop fabric in alternating colors, leave a length of yarn for joining.

Scallop fabric

The simple scallop shown opposite can be repeated to make a fabric. This is done by adding one scallop to the top of another to form strips which are in turn joined by sewing along the sides. The instructions show the scallops being worked in alternating colors. If you are using only one color do not leave long ends of yarn. It is much easier in this case to use a separate length of yarn for joining.

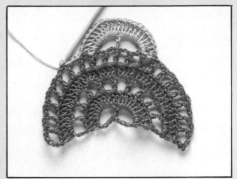

1 Work the first scallop (opposite). Then begin the 2nd scallop on the WS of the first scallop using a new color. Work 1 single crochet into the 2nd double before the center (11th) double. Make 4 chains, skip 1 double, work double into the center double, 4 chains, skip 1 double, 1 single crochet into the next double, finishing slip stitch over next chain and turn into the next double.

2 Turn (RS) and work 10 doubles into the 4-chain space, 1 double into the double, 10 doubles into the next 4-chain space, slip stitch into the next double on first scallop, finishing slip stitch over next 2 chains and into the next double.

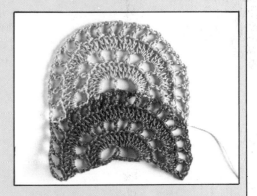

3 Turn and work 2 chains and 1 double into the 3rd double. Work 2 chains, skip 1 double, 1 double into next double all across the row, finishing 2 chains, slip stitch into the next double on first scallop, slip stitch over next 2 chains and then into the next double.

4 Turn and work 3 doubles into each 2-chain space and 1 double into each double to the end of the row, finishing 3 doubles into last 2-chain space, slip stitch into the next double on first scallop, slip stitch over next 2 chains and into the next double.

5 Turn and work the next row in the same way as in 3 but omit the last 3 slip stitches. This completes the 2nd scallop. Leave a long end for joining, then begin the next scallop.

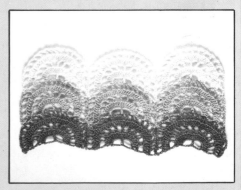

6 Continue making scallops in different colors, following steps 1-5, until the desired length is reached. Then start the next strip and work it in the same color sequence.

7 Make the required number of strips. Using the loose end of yarn on each scallop join the strips together by overcasting on the wrong side, catching in only the back loop of each stitch.

8 Start a new length of yarn with each pair of scallops so that the joining yarn always matches the scallops being sewn together. Join all the strips in the same way.

Fred Mancini

Single scallop edging

Single scallops can be attached side by side to the edge of a fabric as a finishing border. The edging shown in Step 1 is made by working single scallops following the pattern above but varying the size by working only 3 rows for the smallest scallop, 4 rows for the medium-sized scallop and all 5 rows for the largest scallop. The shape of this scallop is especially suited to a curved edge such as a collar or a scalloped edge.

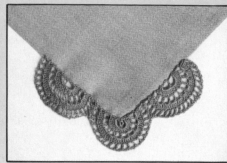

1 To attach the scallops to a straight edge first choose a strong thread which is fine enough to go through your fabric easily. Match the color to the color of the fabric. Overcast the scallops to the WS of the work.

2 When attaching scallops to a shaped edge, lay the scallops around th edge, then overcast the scallops on the WS of the work. Join the scallops together where they touch. Sew to a scalloped edge in the same way.

Stitch Wise

Daffodil

Worked in 3 colors, coded as A, B and C. Using A, make 4ch. Join into a circle with a sl st.
1st round 2ch to count as first hdc, 5hdc into circle. Join with a sl st to 2nd of first 2ch. 6hdc. Join in B.
2nd round Using B, *7ch, 1sc into 3rd ch from hook, 1sc into each of next 5ch (5sc), 1 sl st into next sc, 1sc into next sc, rep from * to end. Join with a sl st to first ch. 3 petals. Turn.
3rd round 1ch to count as first sc, 1sc into each of next 5sc working into back loop only of each st up side of petal, *(1sc, 1ch, 1sc) into top of petal, 6sc down side of petal, working into back loop only of each st, rep from * once more, 6sc down side of last petal, skip sl st and last sc. Join with a sl st to first ch. Work into back loop only of each st from now on.
4th round 1 ch to count as first sc, *1sc into each sc to top of petal, (1sc, 2ch, 1sc) into 1 ch sp at top, 1sc into each sc

to bottom of petal, skip 2 sts at base, rep from * 3 times more. Join with a sl st to first ch.
5th round As 4th. Fasten off.
This completes one petal section. Make another section in the same way.
6th round With ridged side of flower facing and using C work under both loops of each st from now on in usual way, rejoin C to one hdc at center of one petal section, 1 ch to count as first sc, 1sc into st at base of ch, 2sc into each hdc all around.
7th round *1ch to count as first sc, 1sc into each sc to end. Join with a sl st to first ch.
8th round 1ch to count as first sc, 1sc into st at base of ch, *1sc into each of next 2sc, 2sc into next sc, rep from * to last 2 sts, 1 sc into each of next 2 sts. Join with a sl st to first ch.
9th round As 6th.
10th round 2ch to count as first sc and picot point. 1 sl st into 2nd ch from hook, *1sc into next sc, 1ch, 1 sl st into top of st just worked, rep from * to end. Join with a sl st to first ch. Fasten off.
Sew the second petal section to the first so that the petals lie between petals of first section.

Poppy

Worked in 2 colors, A and B. With A, make 6ch. Join into a circle with a sl st.
1st round 1ch, 7sc into circle. 8sc. Join with a sl st to first ch.
2nd round 1ch, *2sc into next sc, rep from * to end. Join with a sl st to first ch. 17sc.
3rd round 1ch, 16sc into circle, working into circle over first 2 rounds. Join with a

sl st to first ch. Cut off A. Join in B.
4th round (petal) **1ch, 1sc into each of next 4sc, turn, *1ch, sc into st at base of ch, 1sc into each sc, 2sc into turning ch *, turn, rep from * to * once more, (9sc), work 2 rows straight on these sc, turn, 1sc, work 2sc tog, 1sc into each of next 3sc, 2sc tog, 1sc into turning ch, turn, 1ch, 2sc tog, 1sc into next sc, 2sc tog, 1sc into turning ch, turn, omit 1ch and first sc, 1sc into each of next 2sc, 2sc tog. Cut yarn.
Make 3 more petals in same way, rep from ** to ** beg each petal in same place as last st of last petal and working last sc of last petal into same place as first on first petal.
5th round 1ch, 1sc into each st all around petal. Cut off B.
6th round (stamens) Rejoin A around stem of any sc worked in last center round, *6ch, sl st into 2nd ch and each ch to center, sc around stem of next sc, rep from * to end. Join with a sl st to first ch.

Four towel edgings

Make one or all of these pretty edgings from crochet cotton and sew them to your towels to add elegance and luxury to bathtime.

Michael Boys

Simon Butcher

First edging

Size
Depth of edging, approx 3in (7.5cm).

Materials
Approx 170yd (155m) of a lightweight mercerized crochet cotton makes two edgings for a towel 16in (41cm) wide
No. 7 (1.50mm) steel crochet hook

Gauge
One section measures approx 2¾in (7cm). For an edging measuring more or less than 16in (41cm), divide the length required by 2¾in (7cm) for the number of sections needed.

Section
Using No. 7 (1.50mm) hook make 13ch.
1st row 1dc into 9th ch from hook, 4ch, 1sc into last ch. Turn.
2nd row 3ch, 9dc into 4ch sp, 1dc into next dc, 9dc all into last ch sp, 1dc into 5th of the 8ch. Turn.
3rd row 5ch, 1dc into 3rd dc, (2ch, skip next dc, 1dc into next dc) to end, working last dc into top of 3ch. Turn. (10sps.)
4th row 3ch, (3dc all into next 2ch sp, 1dc into next dc) to end, finishing 3dc all

into last ch sp, 1dc into 3rd of the 5ch. Turn. 41dc.

5th row As 3rd. 20 sps. Fasten off, leaving a long end for joining sections. This completes first scallop.
With WS of first scallop facing, work 1sc into the dc two to the right of the center dc, 4ch, 1dc into center dc, 4ch, skip next dc, 1sc into next dc, sl st over next 2ch and into next dc, turn.
2nd row Work 10dc all into next 4ch sp, 1dc into next dc, 10dc all into next 4ch sp, sl st into next dc on first scallop, sl st over next 2ch and into next dc, turn. 21dc.
3rd row 2ch, 1dc into dc, (2ch, skip next dc, 1dc into next dc) 8 times, 2ch, sl st into next dc on first scallop, sl st over next 2ch and into next dc, turn.
4th row 3dc into next 2ch sp, (1dc into next dc, 3dc into next 2ch sp) to end, sl st into next dc on first scallop, sl st over next 2ch and into next dc, turn.
5th row 2ch, 1dc into 3rd dc, (2ch, skip next dc, 1dc into next dc) 18 times, 2ch, sl st into next dc on first scallop. Fasten off, leaving a long end for joining sections. This completes one section. Make 5 more sections (or desired length) and join tog for the length of 7 sps.
Work 1 row of sc along top edge.
Make another edging in the same way.
Sew edgings to each end of towel.

Second edging

Size Depth of edging, approx 2¾in (cm).

Materials
Approx 133yd (125m) of a lightweight mercerized crochet cotton makes two edgings for a towel 16in (41cm) wide
No. 7 (1.50mm) steel crochet hook

Gauge
One section measures approx 3¼in (8cm). For an edging measuring more or less than 16in (41cm), divide the length required by 3¼in (8cm) for the number of sections needed.

Section
Using No. 7 (1.50mm) hook make 17ch.
1st row 1dc into 6th ch from hook, 2ch, skip next 2ch, 1dc into each of next 6ch, 2ch, skip next 2ch, 1dc into last ch. Turn.
2nd row 5ch, 1dc into first dc, 2ch, 1dc into each of next 6dc, 2ch, 1dc into last dc. Turn.

3rd–5th rows As 2nd.
6th row 5ch, 1dc into first dc, 2ch, 1dc into each of next 2dc, 1hdc into each of next 2 sts, 1sc into each of next 2sts. Turn.
7th row 1ch, 1sc into each of next 2 sts, 1hdc into each of next 2 sts, 1dc into each of next 2 sts, 2ch, 1dc into last dc. Turn.
8th–17th rows Rep 6th and 7th rows 5 times.
18th row 5ch, 1dc into first dc, 2ch, 1dc into each of next 2 sts, 1hdc into each of next 2 sts, 1sc into each of next 2 sts, 5ch, sl st into last inside 5ch loop on first side of section, turn.
19th row 2ch, 1dc into 3rd of the 5ch, 2ch, 1dc into each of next 2sc, 1dc into each of next 2hdc, 1dc into each of next 2dc, 2ch, 1dc into last dc. Turn.
20th row 5ch, 1dc into first dc, 2ch, 1dc into each of next 6sts, 2ch, 1dc into last dc, 2ch, sl st into next inside loop, turn.
21st row 2ch, 1dc into first dc, 2ch, 1dc into each of next 6 sts, 2ch, 1dc into last dc. Turn.
22nd row As 21st.
23rd row As 22nd.
This completes first section. Do not fasten off, but work 22ch, turn.
Next row 1dc into 6th ch from hook, 2ch, skip next 2ch, 1dc into each of next 6ch, 2ch, skip next 2ch, 1dc into next ch, turn leaving 5ch as joining between first and 2nd sections. Now rep 2nd to 23rd rows as first section, but join outside loops to previous section for first 3 loops thus: at end of next row work 2ch, sl st into loop on previous section, 2ch, turn and omit 5ch at beg of next row.
Cont to make sections in this way until there are 5 sections in all. Fasten off.
Make another edging in the same way.
Sew edgings to each end of towel.

Third edging

Size Depth of edging, approx 2¼in (6cm).

Materials
165yd (150m) of a lightweight mercerized crochet cotton makes two edgings for a towel 16in (41cm) wide
No. 7 (1.50mm) steel crochet hook

To make
Using No. 7 (1.50mm) hook make 16ch, sl st into first ch to form a circle.
1st row 1ch, 1sc into first ch, 2sc into each of next 12ch. Turn, leaving 3ch unworked. 25sc.
2nd row 1ch, 1sc into each sc to end. Turn.
3rd row As 2nd.
4th row 1ch, 1sc into each of first 3sc, (1sc into next sc, 4ch, 1sc into same sc, 1sc into each of next 2sc) 7 times, 1sc into last sc. Turn.
5th row 13ch, sl st into 2nd 4ch loop, turn.
6th row 1ch, 1sc into first ch, 2sc into

each of next 12ch, turn. 25sc.
7th and 8th rows As 2nd.
9th row As 4th.
10th row As 5th.
11th row As 6th.
12th row As 2nd.
13th row As 2nd, then sl st into 3rd 4ch loop of adjacent motif, turn.
The 9th to 13th rows form patt. Rep them for 16in (41cm); end with a 9th row. Fasten off. Join "loose" edges of end shells to adjacent shells. Make another edging in same way. Sew edgings to each end of towel.

Fourth edging

Size Depth of edging, approx 2in (5cm).

Materials
115yd (105m) of a lightweight crochet cotton makes two edgings for a towel 16in (41cm) wide
No. 7 (1.50mm) steel crochet hook

Gauge
One shell section measures approx 3¼in (8cm). For an edging measuring more or less than 16in (41cm), divide the length required by 3¼in (8cm) for the number of shell sections needed, then multiply number of sections by 24, plus 5 for starting ch.

To make
Using No. 7 (1.50mm) hook make 125ch.
1st row 1sc into 2nd ch from hook, 1sc into each ch to end. Turn.
2nd row 5ch, 1dc into 4th sc, (2ch, skip next 2sc, 1dc into next sc) to end. Turn. 41 sps.
3rd row 1ch, 1sc into first dc, (2sc into next 2ch sp, 1sc into next dc) 7 times. Turn. 22sc.
4th row 16ch, skip first 7sc, 1sc into next sc, turn. 8sc into 16ch sp, 1sc into 8th of the 16ch, turn, *10ch, 1sc into same sc on 3rd row, turn, 8sc into 10ch sp, 1sc into 8th of the 10ch, turn*, rep from * to * once more, 8ch, skip next 6sc on 3rd row, 1sc into next sc, turn.
5th row 11sc into next 8ch sp, 1sc into top of first branch, (4sc into next 2ch sp, 1sc into top of next branch) twice, 11sc into next 8ch sp, 2sc into next 2ch sp on 2nd row, 1sc into next dc, turn.
6th row 1dc into each of next 33sc around shell, sl st into 3rd sc on 3rd row, turn.
7th row sl st over first 4dc, (sl st into next dc, 4ch, sl st into same dc, sl st over next 5dc) 5 times, working over 4dc instead of 5dc at end of last rep. Fasten off.
This completes one shell section.
Rejoin yarn to next st on 2nd row and rep 3rd to 7th rows again.
Cont in this way until 5 shells are completed. Rejoin yarn to next st on 2nd row and work 2sc into end 5ch sp, 1sc into 3rd of the 5ch. Fasten off.
Make another edging in the same way.
Sew edgings to each end of towel.

Crochet / COURSE 85

Combining different yarns

Interesting textures can be achieved by working two yarns simultaneously, using one of the many bulky or unusual textured yarns available today, together with a plainer knitting worsted. By weaving the thicker or textured yarn through the stitches being worked in the finer yarn, it is possible to create very individual fabrics, as the whole appear-

ance of the crochet will be determined by the combination of yarns being used.
The fabric may be created in two ways. The first method is to strand the yarn across the work in the same way as in working a colored pattern, but working across the front rather than the back of it. Alternatively, the thicker yarn can be woven in and out of the background fabric by

taking it to the front and then to the back of the fabric either after each stitch has been worked or after several stitches have been worked for a more widely spaced effect. This method creates a fairly thick fabric which can be used either as an allover pattern for a complete garment or to highlight points in your design.

The stranding method

Single crochet or half doubles should be used for the background fabric for the best results, since the yarn, when taken across a double or triple crochet fabric, lies at the bottom of the stitches, leaving the upper part uncovered and so producing a rather open fabric.
The technique can be used to highlight a particular point of a garment, using a contrasting color for the stranding yarn if desired, or it can be worked as a complete pattern all over a garment, using two tones or shades of one color for a subtler effect.
When working in this way choose a hook which is suitable for the plain background yarn, rather than for the thicker stranded yarn, so that you obtain a firm, even crochet fabric.

1 Our sample has been worked in half doubles to make a fairly light crochet background, but you could use single crochet, if preferred, for a more closely woven effect. Use a plain knitting worsted, as shown on the left, and a thick mohair-type yarn, as shown on the right, with a size H (5.00mm) hook.

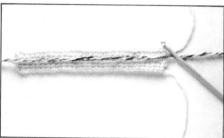

2 Work three half double rows with the plain yarn. Now hold the textured yarn at the right-hand edge of the work, with the cut end to the right so that the working end lies across the fabric.

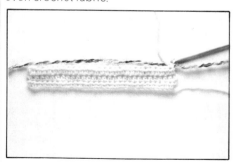

3 Work the first turning chain over the cut end to hold it in place at the side of the fabric.

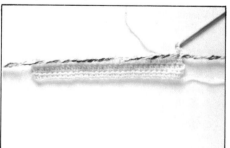

4 Work one more turning chain then a half double into the 2nd stitch in the normal way, holding the textured yarn at the front of the work so that it lies flat against it.

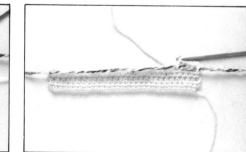

5 Work into next two stitches in the normal way, holding the textured yarn across the fabric. On the next stitch, work over the textured yarn at the same time to hold it in place. The number of stitches worked between the "catching" stitches can be varied according to the effect desired.

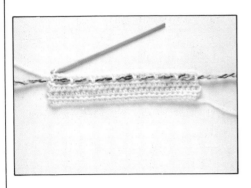

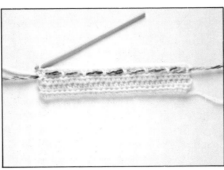

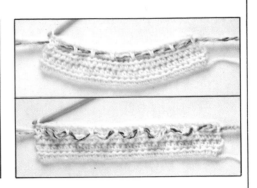

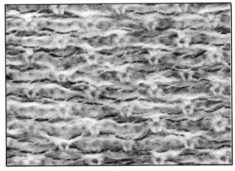

6 Continue to work across the row in this way, catching the textured yarn into the background fabric while working every following 4th stitch.

7 Work over the yarn at the end of the row while working into the top of the turning chain in the previous row, so that the yarn is held firmly in place at the edge of the work.

8 Make sure that the yarn is held firmly but evenly across the work. If it is held too loosely against the fabric it will tend to loop downward (see lower photograph) making an untidy fabric. Conversely, if held too tightly it will pull the background fabric out of shape (see top photograph).

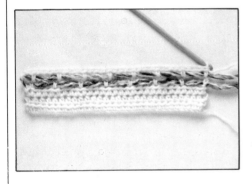

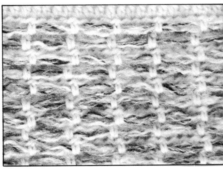

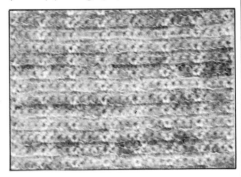

9 Turn and hold the textured yarn at the back of the work. Make one turning chain, working over the textured yarn to bring it up to the correct level. Make one more chain. Now work as before, catching the yarn in place while working every 4th stitch. Here we show the 2nd row completed on the RS of the work.

10 Work in the same way on every row to obtain a closely woven fabric with the textured yarn creating a raised effect on the front of the crochet.

11 Here the same method has been used on a single crochet background, combining plain knitting worsted and an unusual bouclé yarn.

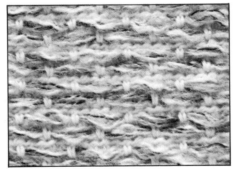

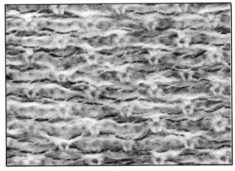

12 For a more spaced effect work two or more plain rows between each stranded or woven row. In this case you should cut the textured yarn at the end of each stranded row and rejoin it once more when it is needed.

13 The same method can be varied to create a "brick" effect. In this case you work an uneven number of stitches in each block. Hold the yarn across the work as before, but work over the textured yarn on every 5th stitch. On the following row work into the center of each 5-stitch block. It will be necessary to work half blocks at each end of the row to create the correct pattern.

14 Use the same method for a wider pattern, working two or more rows in the same position before altering the brick sequence as shown here.

The weaving method

In this method a more tightly woven effect is achieved by weaving the yarn in and out of the stitches while working across the row. Either single crochet or half doubles should be used; the first makes a very close, thick fabric and the second a more widely spaced woven effect.

This method is ideal for making an entire garment for which a thick, soft texture is required. When working the shaping on a garment, work in the background yarn only, shaping at the edge in the normal way, but making sure that the textured yarn is carried to the edge of the work each time to ensure a neat finish to the garment.

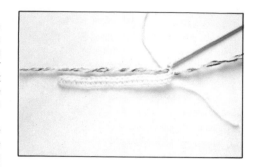

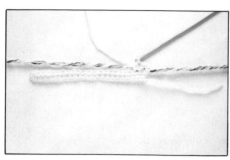

1 Work one half double row. Now hold the cut end of the textured yarn at the back of the work on the right-hand side, bringing it through to the front between the turning chain and the first stitch.

2 Work the next stitch with the yarn held at the front of the work. Now take the textured yarn to the back of the work and crochet the next stitch in the normal way.

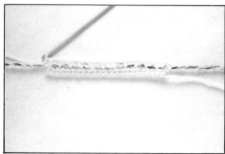

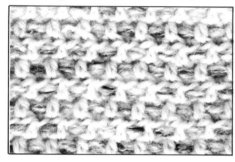

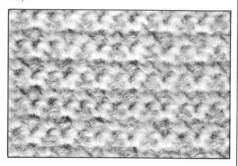

3 Continue to weave the yarn in and out of the stitches to the end of the row. Where the yarn lies at the back at the end of the row, turn and take it around the edge of the work to the back, then through to the front as before. Where it lies at the front of the work at the end of the row, turn and bring it through to the front as before.

4 Continue to work in the same way on every row, taking the yarn to the back of the work and through to the front again after every stitch each time and completing each row as before. For a more widely spaced pattern take the yarn to the back or front after every 2nd or 3rd stitch.

5 For a more closely woven fabric work in single crochet, as shown here, rather than half doubles. Choose soft yarns when working in single crochet to obtain a lightly woven effect.

Fabric textures

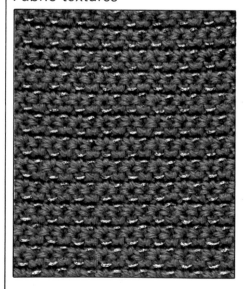

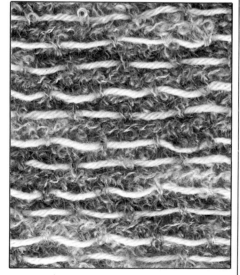

Knitting worsted woven with glitter   *Knitting worsted stranded with a Shetland yarn*   *Bouclé stranded with knitting worsted*

Stitch Wise

Colored cross-doubles pattern

Use two colors, coded here as A and B. Make a multiple of 4 chains plus 1.
1st row Using A, 2dc into 5th ch from hook, *skip 1ch, 2dc into next ch, rep from * to end. Turn.
2nd row Using A, 2ch, *work (1dc, 1ch, 1dc) between next 2dc grp of first row, rep from * to end, 1dc into top of turning ch. Turn.
3rd row Using B, 2ch, yo, insert hook into center of first 2dc grp of first row, yo and draw through a long loop, yo and draw through 2 loops on hook, yo and insert hook into sp before first 2dc grp of first row, yo and draw through a loop, yo and draw through 2 loops, yo and draw through rem loops on hook — called 2 crossed doubles (2crdc) —, work 2crdc group in same way into each 2dc grp worked in first row to end, 1sc into 2nd of turning ch. Turn.
4th row Using B, 2ch, * (1dc, 1ch, 1dc) into next 1ch sp between 2dc worked in 2nd row, rep from * to end, 1dc into top

of turning ch. Turn.
5th row Using A, 2ch, yo and insert hook into sp at left of first 2crdc group worked in 3rd row, yo and draw through a loop, yo and draw through 2 loops on hook, yo and insert hook into sp at right of first 2crdc group worked in 3rd row, yo and draw through a loop, yo and draw through 2 loops on hook, yo and draw through rem loops on hook, *yo and insert hook into sp at left of next 2crdc group worked in 3rd row, yo and draw through a loop, yo and draw through 2 loops on hook, yo and insert hook into same place as first dc in previous 2crdc group in same row, complete 2crdc group as before, rep from * to end, 1sc into top of turning ch. Turn.
6th row Using A, 2ch, *(1dc, 1ch, 1dc) into 1ch sp between next 2dc worked in 4th row, rep from * to end, 1dc into top of turning ch. Turn.
Rep 5th and 6th rows for pattern, working two rows in each color and working into the row preceding row just worked each time.

Colored shell and raised-doubles pattern

Use two colors, coded as A and B. Break off each color at end of row every time and rejoin at beg of appropriate row. Begin by making a multiple of 8 chains plus 7.
1st row 1dc into 4th ch from hook, 1dc into each of next 3ch, *skip 1ch, work (2dc, 2ch, 2dc) into next ch — called 1 shell — skip 1ch, 1dc into each of next 5ch, rep from * to end. Break off A. Join in B.
2nd row Using B, 2ch, skip first dc, 1dc around stem of each of next 4dc, taking hook from front around back and to front again — called 1 double front (1dcF) —, *work 1 shell into 2ch sp at center of next shell, 1dcF around stem of each of next 5dc, rep from * to end, working last dc into top of turning ch. Turn. Break off B.
Join in A.
Rep 2nd row for pattern, changing color on every row.

Man's bulky jacket

Highlight the shoulders of a lovely warm cardigan by weaving in a contrasting yarn.

Sizes
To fit 38[40:42]in (97[102:107]cm) chest.
Length, 27¾[28¼:29]in (71[72:74]cm).
Sleeve seam, 18[18½:19]in (46[47:48]cm), excluding cuff.
Note Directions for larger sizes are in brackets [ ]; if there is only one set of figures it applies to all sizes.

Materials
38[39:41]oz (1050[1100:1150]g) of a knitting worsted
4oz (100g) of a bulky novelty yarn
Size H (5.00mm) crochet hook
8 buttons

Gauge
14hdc and 10 rows to 4in (10cm) worked on size H (5.00mm) hook.

Back
Using size H (5.00mm) hook and knitting worsted make 79[81:85]ch.
Base row 1hdc into 3rd ch from hook, 1hdc into each ch to end. Turn. 78[80:84] sts.
Patt row 2ch to count as first hdc, skip first hdc, 1hdc into each hdc to end, 1hdc into top of 2ch. Turn.
Rep patt row until work measures 18in (46cm). Cont in hdc weaving in novelty yarn on first and every 4th st on first row and 3rd and every 4th st on 2nd row — foll step-by-step instructions on page 12 — to end of back.
Shape armholes
Sl st across first 3[3:4]sts, sl st into next st, 2ch, 1hdc into each st to within last 3[3:4]sts, turn.
Next row 2ch, skip first hdc, (yo, insert

hook in next st and draw a loop through) twice, yo, draw through all loops on hook — called decrease 1 or dec 1 —, 1hdc into each hdc to within last 3sts, dec 1, 1hdc in top of 2ch. Turn. Rep last row 3 times more. 64[66:68]sts. Cont in patt straight until armholes measure 9¾[10¼:11]in (25[26:28]cm).
Shape shoulders
Sl st across first 7sts, sl st into next st, 2ch, 1hdc into each hdc to within last 7sts, turn.
Next row Sl st across first 6sts, sl st into next st, 2ch, 1hdc into each hdc to within last 6sts, turn.
Rep last row once more. 26[28:30]sts. Fasten off.

Left front
Using size H (5.00mm) hook make

Chris Harvey

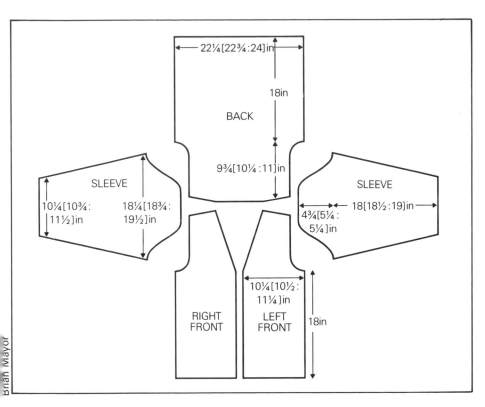

BACK — 22¼[22¾:24]in — 18in

9¾[10¼:11]in

SLEEVE — 10¼[10¾:11½]in — 18¼[18¾:19½]in

SLEEVE — 18[18½:19]in — 4¾[5¼:5¼]in

RIGHT FRONT

LEFT FRONT — 10¼[10½:11¼]in — 18in

Brian Mayor

37[38.40]ch and work base row as for back. 36[37:39] sts. Work in patt as for back until work measures same as back to armholes. Cont in hdc weaving in novelty yarn on first and every 4th st on first row and 3rd and every 4th st on 2nd row—foll step-by-step instructions on page 12—to end of front.

Shape armhole
Sl st across first 3[3:4]sts, sl st into next st, 2ch, 1hdc into each hdc to within last 3sts, dec 1 (for front neck edge), 1hdc into top of 2ch. Turn.
Next row Patt to within last 3sts, dec 1, 1 hdc into top of 2ch. Turn.
Next row 2ch, skip first hdc, dec 1, patt to within last 3sts, dec 1, 1 hdc into top of 2ch. Turn.
Rep last 2 rows until 4 decs have been made at armhole edge. Keeping armhole edge straight cont to dec one st at neck edge on every other row until 19 sts rem. Cont straight until front measures same as back; end at armhole edge.

Shape shoulder
Sl st across first 7sts, sl st into next st, 2ch, work to end. Turn.
Next row Work to within last 6sts, fasten off.

Right front
Work as left front reversing shapings.

Sleeves
Using size H (5.00mm) hook make 37[39:41]ch and work base row as for back. 36[38:40]sts. Cont in patt as for back, inc one st at each end of every 3rd row until there are 64[66:68]sts. Cont straight until sleeve measures 18[18½:19]in (46[47:48]cm). Cont in hdc weaving

in novelty yarn on first and every 4th st on first row and 3rd and every 4th st on 2nd row—foll step-by-step instructions on page 12—to end of sleeve.

Shape top
Work first row of back armhole shaping.
Next row Sl st into first st, sl st into next st, 2ch, 1 hdc into each st to within last st, turn.
Rep last row until 36 sts rem. Fasten off.

Button band
Using size H (5.00mm) hook and knitting worsted, make 12ch.
Base row Sl st into 4th ch from hook, * 1dc into next ch, sl st into next ch, rep from * to end. Turn. 10sts.
Patt row 3ch, skip first sl st,* sl st into next dc, 1dc into next sl st, rep from * to within last 3ch, sl st into top of 3ch. Turn.
1st buttonhole row 3ch, skip first sl st, sl st into next dc, 1dc into next sl st, sl st into next dc, 2ch, skip next 2sts, 1dc in next sl st, sl st into next dc, 1dc into next

sl st, sl st into top of 3ch. Turn.
2nd buttonhole row 3ch, skip first sl st, sl st into next dc, 1dc into next sl st, sl st into next dc, 1dc into next ch, sl st into next ch, 1dc into next sl st, sl st into next dc, 1dc into next sl st, sl st into top of 3ch. Turn.
Now rep patt row 6 times.
Rep the last 8 rows 7 more times, then cont in patt only until band, when slightly stretched, fits up left front, around neck, and down right front. Fasten off.

Collar
Using size H (5.00mm) hook and knitting worsted, make 25ch and work base row as for front band. 24sts. Now work in patt as for band until collar measures 24in (61cm). Fasten off.

Pockets (make two)
Using size H (5.00mm) hook and knitting worsted, make 25ch and work base row and patt row as for back. Work in patt as for back until pocket measures 3½in (9cm).
Next row 3ch, skip first hdc, *sl st into next hdc, 1dc into next hdc, rep from * to within last 2ch, sl st into top of 2ch. Turn. Now work in patt as for front band until pocket measures 6in (15cm). Fasten off.

Cuffs
Using size H (5.00mm) hook and knitting worsted, and working into base row of sleeves, work 28[30:32]sc.
Next row 3ch, skip first sc, sl st into next sc, *1dc into next sc, sl st into next sc, rep from * to end. Turn.
Now work in patt as for front band for 3in (7.5cm). Fasten off.

To finish
Press or block according to yarn used. Join shoulder, side and sleeve seams. Set in sleeves. Pin front band in place, easing to fit, then sew in place. Place center back of collar inside front band, to match center back neck edge of jacket, sew down collar, then turn up and over front bands to outside. Sew on pockets. Sew on buttons.

Crochet / COURSE 86

* Three-dimensional crochet
* Making and stuffing simple shapes
* Pattern for three airplanes

Three-dimensional crochet

There are many ways in which crochet pieces, sewn together and stuffed with fiberfill, foam chips or blocks, or other suitable filling, can be used.

Practical items such as large, bright-colored crochet cubes made from crochet squares and filled with foam blocks can make simple but attractive stools for a child's bedroom; a long cylindrical shape made by working a tubular fabric (see Volume 4, page 11), and stuffing it firmly with fiberfill or foam chips makes an ideal draft stopper, which, with the addition of crochet or felt features, can be colorful and fun too.

Toys, which can be made from simple square or circular shapes, or from shaped pieces, demonstrate perfectly the versatility of this technique, since the use of different colored or textured yarns together with the addition of different features can alter the basic look considerably.

With the imaginative use of color and shapes, combined with the many different crochet techniques learned so far, you should be able to make a number of different items successfully.

Begin by making something really simple like a child's toy, using only squares or circles, which can be crocheted freehand from a basic drawing. By starting in this way, you will discover for yourself the most suitable ways of stuffing the various pieces and how best to sew them together.

Once you have mastered the technique, you will be able to progress quite easily to something more complicated, such as the airplane mobile featured on page 20, or to create your own designs. If several different-shaped pieces are to be used to make a large, complicated object, you should plan your design on graph paper with the help of a stitch gauge square to achieve the correct shape and determine where increasing and decreasing should occur.

Making and stuffing simple shapes

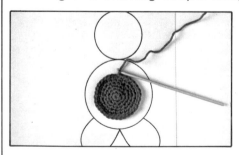

1 Whether you are making a simple toy or something more complicated, you should draw the basic shape on plain paper first, making it the size of the finished article if possible, or draw it to scale on graph paper. If only circles or squares are being used, the crochet can be worked without instructions by using the paper picture as a guide and placing the crochet on the paper shape from time to time until it is the required size.

2 Use any yarn which you may have left over from previous projects to begin with, using bright colors where possible if you are working only basic shapes. Subtle color combinations are best used in more complicated pieces. Work in single crochet or half doubles for a firm fabric, which will prevent the stuffing from showing.

3 Any additional features should be made and sewn to the appropriate pieces before the main pieces are joined. You can use crochet circles, ovals and strips to make the features, or try pieces of felt if you like. If possible, use the same yarn to sew the pieces in place. If this is not practical, choose a yarn that will hold the features firmly in place.

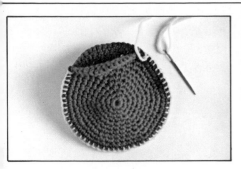

4 Place the wrong side of the two pieces together and overcast all around, leaving a small gap at the top for the stuffing. To make a feature of the joining, use a contrasting yarn and crochet the two pieces together, or use a more decorative stitch. Here we have used blanket stitch for a firm but decorative joining. Make sure that the pieces are joined together firmly.

5 For a small object like the one shown here, fiberfill, bits of yarn or pieces of old pantyhose or stockings could be used for stuffing. Larger objects will need something firmer, such as plastic foam chips or blocks, for the best results. The shape of the object can be altered considerably, depending on how firmly the pieces are stuffed.

6 Finally sew the remaining gap together to complete each section. You may find it necessary to mold the sphere into shape once it has been completed to distribute the stuffing evenly and obtain a good shape.

7 Sew the two pieces together firmly, using the same yarn as the main section if possible. Work as neatly as possible at the base of the top section so that the stitches are invisible.
Flatter pieces like the wings of the airplane featured on page 18 may be more difficult to sew neatly in place. In this case you can use a finer yarn if necessary.

8 Some additional features, such as the airplane wings or hands or feet, may need strengthening. Ordinary stuffing would not be suitable, and in this case it is advisable to use thick cardboard, which can be cut to shape using the crochet piece as a pattern.

9 Overcast the pieces together with the wrong sides facing, leave a gap one side into which the cardboard strengthener can be inserted. Then close the gap completely.

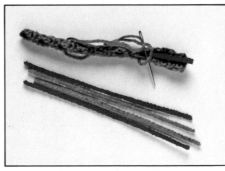

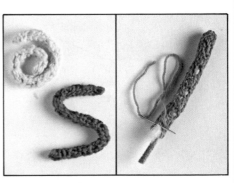

10 The piece can then be sewn in place, catching the crochet only to the main section of the stuffed item.

11 Pipe cleaners can be used to strengthen narrow pieces. Crochet the length required and fold it around the pipe cleaner, bending the end upward and twisting it around the stem to prevent a sharp point. Overcast the two pieces together, taking the needle through the pipe cleaner at each end to hold the fabric in place.

12 The strips can then be twisted to make the desired shape. Larger pieces can also be strengthened in the same way, placing the pipe cleaner at the center of the crochet and placing the stuffing all around as shown.

Fred Mancini

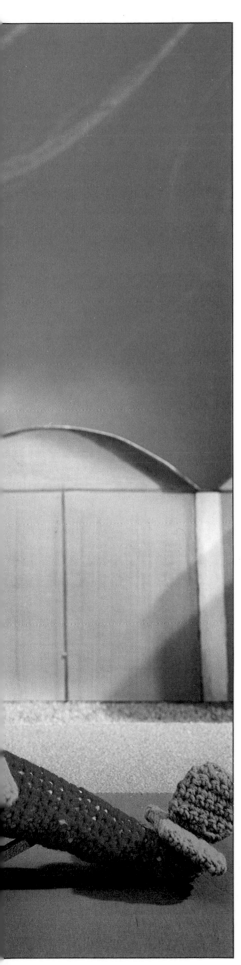

Three airplanes

Fasten your seat belts—our airplanes are landing. They make a super mobile too.

Size Length, approx 9½in (24cm).

Materials
For each airplane allow:
2oz (40g) of a sport yarn in main color (A)
2oz (40g) in contrasting color (B)
Small amount in contrasting color (C)
Size E (3.50mm) crochet hook
Cardboard; wood glue
Balsa wood dowels
Chenille yarn for propeller

Monoplane

Body
Using size E (3.50mm) hook and A, make 21ch.
Base row 2sc into 2nd ch from hook, 1sc into each of next 4sc, *2sc into next sc, 1sc into each of next 4sc, rep from * to end. Turn.
1st-5th rows 1ch, 1sc into each sc to end. Turn.
6th row 1ch, work next 2sc tog, 1sc into each sc to within last 2sc, work last 2sc tog. Turn.
7th-9th rows 1ch, 1sc into each sc to end. Turn.
Rep last 4 rows 6 times more. 10sc.
Next row 1ch, 1sc into each sc to end. Turn.
Next row 1ch, *work next 2sc tog, rep from * once more, 1sc into each of next 6sc. Turn. 8sc.
Next row 1ch, 1sc into each sc to end. Turn.
Next row 1ch, work next 2sc tog, 1sc into next sc, work next 2sc tog, 1sc into each of next 3sc. Fasten off.
Using size E (3.50mm) hook and A, make 4ch, sl st into first ch to form a circle.
1st round 1ch, work 7sc into circle, sl st into first sc.
2nd round 1ch, 1sc into sl st, *2sc into next sc, 1sc into next sc, rep from * twice more, 2sc into last sc, sl st into first sc. 12sc.
3rd round As 2nd. 18sc. Fasten off.

Wing
Using size E (3.50mm) hook and B, make 45ch.
Base row 1sc into 2nd ch from hook, 1sc into each ch to end. Turn.
1st row 1ch, 1sc into each sc to end. Turn.
2nd row 1ch, 2sc into next sc, 1sc into each sc to within last sc, 2sc into last sc. Turn. 46sc.
3rd and 4th rows As first.

5th row As 2nd. 48sc.
6th-9th rows As first.
Fasten off.
Make another piece in the same way.

Tail
Using size E (3.50mm) hook and B, make 11ch.
Base row 1sc into 2nd ch from hook, 1sc into each ch to end. Turn.
1st row 1ch, 2sc into next sc, 1sc into each sc to within last sc, 2sc into last sc. Turn.
2nd and 3rd rows 1ch, 1sc into each sc to end. Turn. 12sc.
4th row 1ch, 2sc into next sc, 1sc into each of next 5sc. Turn.
5th row 1ch, work next 2sc tog, 1sc into each of next 5sc. Turn.
6th row 1ch, 1sc into each sc to within last 2sc, work last 2sc tog. Fasten off.
Rejoin yarn to center of rem 6sc and work 1sc into each sc to end. Turn.
Work 4th-6th rows once. Fasten off.
Make another piece in the same way.

Rudder
Using size E (3.50mm) hook and B, make 6ch.
Base row 1ch, 1sc into each sc to end. Turn.
1st row 1ch, 1sc into each of next 4sc, 2sc into last sc. Turn.
2nd-4th rows 1ch, 1sc into each sc to end. Turn.
5th row 1ch, 2sc into next sc, 1sc into each sc to end. Turn.
6th row 1ch, work next 2sc tog, 1sc into each of next 3sc, work next 2sc tog. Turn.
7th row 1ch, work next 2sc tog, 1sc into next sc, work next 2sc tog.
Fasten off.
Make another piece in the same way.

Wheels (make 2)
Using size E (3.50mm) hook and C, make 4ch, sl st into first ch to form a circle.
1st round 1ch, work 7sc into circle, sl st into first sc.
2nd round 1ch, 1sc into sl st, *2sc into next sc, 1sc into next sc, rep from * to last sc, 2sc into last sc, sl st into first sc. 12sc.
3rd round As 2nd. 18sc. Fasten off.
Make another piece in the same way.

To finish
Using wing, tail, rudder and wheel as patterns, cut cardboard to shape. Join long seam of body section, stuff firmly, then sew circle in place. Join wing, tail, rudder and wheel sections tog over cardboard. Cut cardboard propeller and wrap it with chenille, gluing while wrapping. Sew to body. Attach wing to body; use balsa wood painted black to form struts and undercarriage. Attach wheels to undercarriage. Sew rudder to tail; sew tail to body.

Biplane

Work as for monoplane, but make 2 wings and join wings together with balsa wood as shown in picture below.

Triplane

Work as for monoplane, but make 3 wings and join them together with balsa wood as shown in the picture on page 18.

Bob Enever

Crochet / COURSE 87

Crochet novelties

By combining the three-dimensional crochet described in the previous issue with pieces of flat crochet, it is possible to make many unusual crochet novelties which can be used both for decoration and for more functional purposes.

The technique relies on your own imagination, ingenuity and skill to create individual items which can be inspired by such things as butterflies, insects and small animals.

We give instructions for a butterfly and moth to be used to decorate a pillow or bedspread and also for a ladybug-shaped pillow, using the body of the ladybug to form the main section of the pillow with the wings and markings providing additional decoration. From these shapes and techniques you can create your own designs.

The best results are obtained by using a firm, close stitch such as single crochet or half doubles, and using color and texture to highlight a particular point or section of your design. The use of different yarns is a simple, but effective, way of emphasizing sections of your design, so that the head of a moth, for example, could be worked in mohair with the body in a plain yarn. Detail can be added either by using textured stitches, or by making crochet circles and strips to be sewn onto the main sections. Embroidery stitches can also be used effectively to make facial features, outline spots or mark divisions on a wing.

Winged insects

1 The body of an insect can be made in several ways. The simplest method is to make a piece of tubular crochet without joining each round, so that the crochet is worked in a spiral. The body is shaped by increasing or decreasing at appropriate points in the tube. (See pattern on page 23.)

2 To make segments, yarn can be tied tightly around a plain, unshaped tube which is filled with cotton or synthetic stuffing to indicate the different sections of the body.

3 Here separate pieces have been made for the head, body and tail and sewn together to make a flexible body.

4 To make feelers, work a length of chains equivalent to the length of **both** feelers. Hold florist's wire against the chain (left), then work single crochet down the length of the chains and over the wire (center). Sew at center to head and curl the ends (right).

5 To make a very small body—for example when making a dragonfly —make a length of chains to the correct size for the completed insect and work single crochet along both sides of the chains, working 3 single crochets into each end.

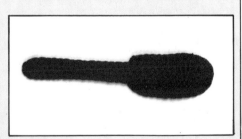

6 To make a wider section, turn at the center of one row and work back to the same point on the other side of the chain. The size of the dragonfly will depend on the number of rows worked this way.

Mike Berend

continued

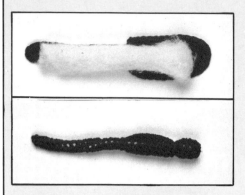

7 Narrow pieces can be difficult to stuff properly. Cut a piece of batting to the correct length and curve the crochet pieces around it before sewing the two edges together. If necessary, double batting at head. Tie thread tightly around wide end to make a head.

8 Dragonfly wings can be made in exactly the same way as the body since they are quite narrow. To make one end flat rather than rounded, turn after both sides of the chains have been covered and work back around the stitches just made. Spray starch could be used to stiffen the wings.

9 If the insect is to be used for decoration, small butterfly wings can be made from a single piece of crochet. To stiffen the wings, work over florist's wire held around the edge of the wing, working single crochet over the wire and into the edge of the wing.

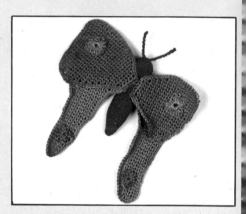

10 Double the wire at the flat side of the wing and twist the two pieces together before working over the wire in single crochet. The ends should be cut as close to the fabric as possible.

11 The wings must be sewn really firmly in place on the body. Overlap the top and lower wings and overcast firmly in place, catching both the underside and top to the body.

12 Additional features or markings can either be worked into the main fabric or sewn onto the wings once they have been completed. Spots in contrasting colors can be made, using small crochet circles, and sewn in place. Sew additional features on **before** the wings are sewn to the body.

13 Embroidery can also be used to make additional markings. French knots worked in contrasting color form small dots as shown here on a ladybug's wings. The ladybug has been made from a circle of crochet, the body divided and outlined with embroidery.

14 Larger wings which are to be used for for something like the pillow featured on page 26 must be firmly constructed. Make two pieces for each wing, using contrasting colors or different kinds of yarn for added interest.

15 Cut a piece of batting to the shape of the wing, using crochet pieces as a guide, and baste the batting to the wrong side of one section. Sew the two crochet pieces together by overcasting neatly all around the edge.

Moth and butterfly

Our moth and butterfly in fine crochet cotton will inspire you to make more busy insects to decorate your home.

Moth

Size
Approx 6¾×5in (13×17cm).

Materials
Approx 150yd (135m) of a lightweight mercerized crochet cotton in variegated brown and in black
Approx 110yd (105m) of a metallic fingering yarn in silver
Size B (2.50mm) crochet hook
Fine wire

Body
Using size B (2.50mm) hook and brown yarn make 4ch, sl st into first ch to form a circle.
Next round 1 ch, 6sc into circle.
Working in continuous rounds, work 1sc into each of next 12sc, (2sc into next sc, 1sc into each of next 3sc) 8 times, 1sc into next sc, place a marker on last sc worked. Work 3 rounds sc.
Join on black. With black work 2 rounds. Now work 3 rounds brown, 2 rounds black and 1 round brown.
Next round With brown, 1sc into next sc, *work next 2sc tog, 1sc into each of next 2sc, rep from * 3 times more, work last 2sc tog. Turn.
Work 2 rounds black. Cut off black. Stuff body firmly. Cont in brown only, work 2 rounds.
Shape for head
*Work 2sc into next sc, 1sc into next sc, rep from * 10 times more. Mark next sc. Work 4 rounds.
Stuff heads firmly, cont to stuff head and dec as foll:
*Work next 2sc tog, 1sc into next sc, rep from * until 3sc rem. Cut off yarn, thread end through rem loop, gather tightly and secure.

Feelers
Using size B (2.50mm) hook and black, make 30ch.
Next row 1sc into 2nd ch from hook, holding a piece of wire against ch work 1sc into each ch to end, working over wire at the same time. Fasten off.

Wings
Working in sc, foll charts, working 2 wings of each shape. Work 1 row of sc in brown around each wing, working over wire at same time. Sew on wings and feelers; sew across center of feelers.

John Hutchinson

Kim Sayer

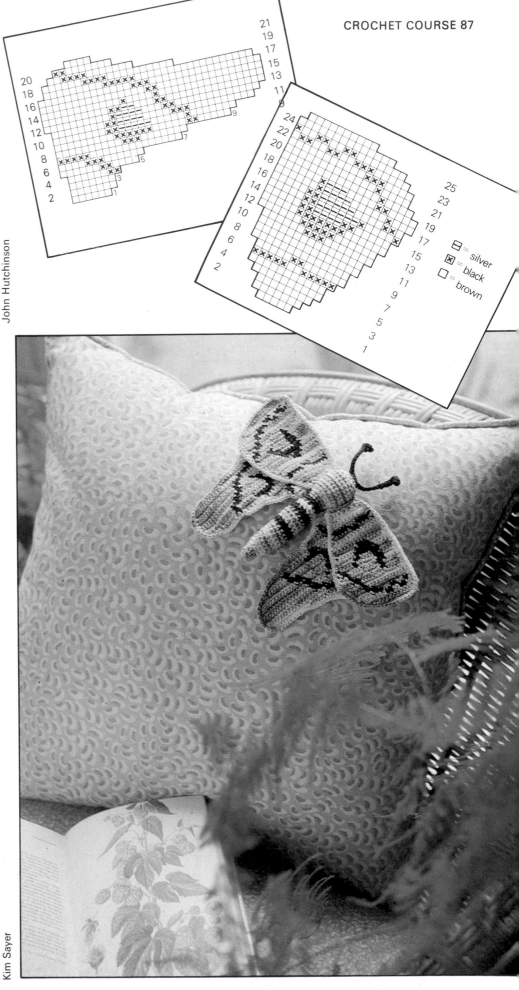

□ = silver
☒ = black
□ = brown

23

Butterfly

Size Approx 7 × 6¾in (17 × 18cm).

Materials
*Approx 150yd (135m) of a
    lightweight crochet cotton
Size B (2.50mm) crochet hook
Fine wire*

Body
Using size B (2.50mm) hook make 4ch,
sl st into first ch to form a circle.
1st round 1ch, 6sc into circle.
Working in continuous rounds, work 1sc
into each of next 12sc, (2sc into next
sc, 1sc into each of next 3sc) 8 times
1sc into next sc, place a marker on
last sc.
Work 18 rounds sc.
Next round 1sc into next sc, *work next
2sc tog, 1sc into each of next 2sc, rep
from * 3 times, work next 2sc tog.
Work 3 rounds. Stuff body firmly.
Shape for head
Work *2sc into next sc, 1sc into next
sc, rep from *10 times more. Mark next
sc. Work 4 rounds.
Stuff head firmly, cont to stuff head
and dec as foll:
*Work next 2sc tog, 1sc into next sc,
rep from * until 3sc rem. Cut off yarn,
thread end through rem loop, gather
tightly and secure.

Feelers
Using size B (2.50mm) hook make 30ch.
Next row 1sc into 2nd ch from hook,
holding a piece of wire against ch work
1sc into each ch to end, working over
wire at same time. Fasten off.

Top wings (make 2)
Using size B (2.50mm) hook make 20ch.
Base row 1sc into 2nd ch from hook,
1sc into each ch to end. Turn.
Next row 1ch, working into back loop
only work 2sc into next sc, 1sc into
each sc to within last sc, 2sc into last
sc. Turn.
Rep last row 4 times more. 29sc.
Work 1 row without shaping.
Next row 3ch, 1dc into next sc, leaving
last loop of each on hook work 6dc all
into next sc, yo and draw a loop
through all loops on hook—cluster
formed—, *1dc into each of next 3sc, 1
cluster into next sc, rep from * 5 times
more, 1dc into each of last 2sc. Turn.
Next row 1ch, 1sc into first dc, *1sc
into top of cluster, 1sc into each of
next 3dc, rep from * to end, working
last sc into top of 3ch. Turn. 29sc.
Next row 4ch, *skip next sc, 1dc into
next sc, 1ch, rep from * to end. Turn.
Next row 1ch, *1sc into first dc, 1sc
into sp, rep from * to end. Turn.
Next row 3ch *skip next sc, 1dc, 2ch
and 1dc all into next sc, skip next sc,
rep from * to end, finishing 1dc into

last sc. Turn.
Next row 1sc into first dc, 3sc into each
sp, 1sc into turning ch. Turn.
Next row 4ch, *skip next 2sc, 1dc into
next sc, 1ch, rep from * to end. Turn.
Next row 1ch, 2sc into each sp to end.
Turn. 18sc.
Next row 3ch, 1dc into next sc, 1 cluster
into next sc, *1dc into each of next 3sc,
1 cluster into next sc, rep from * twice
more, 1dc into each of last 3sc. Turn.
Working into back loop only work 3
rows sc. (Work 1 more row here for
2nd wing.)
Next row 1sc into each of next 12sc,
turn.

Next row 1sc into each sc to end. Turn.
Next row 1sc into each of next 7sc,
turn.
Next row 1sc into each sc to end. Turn.
Work 1 row of sc around outer edge of
wing, working over wire at the same
time. Fasten off.
Make another wing in the same way,
noting the exception in parentheses
above.

Lower wings (make 2)
Using size B (2.50mm) hook make 4ch.
1st row 1sc into 2nd ch from hook, 1sc
into each of next 2ch. Turn.
2nd row 1ch, 2sc into first sc, 1sc into

next sc, 2sc into last sc. Turn.

3rd row 4ch, 1dc into base of 4ch, (1ch, skip next sc, 1dc into next sc) twice, 1ch, 1dc into same place as last dc. Turn.

4th row 1ch, *1sc into first dc, 1sc into next sp, rep from * to end. Turn. 9sc.

5th row 4ch, 1dc into base of 4ch, *skip next 2sc, 1dc, 1ch and 1dc all into next sc, rep from * to within last 2sc, skip next sc, 1dc, 1ch and 1dc all into last sc. Turn.

6th row 1ch, 1sc into first dc, 3sc into each sp to end. Turn. 13sc.

7th row 4ch, 1dc into base of 4ch. *1ch, skip next sc, 1dc into next sc, rep from * to end, 1ch, 1dc into same place as last dc.. Turn.

8th row 1ch, 1sc into first dc, *1sc into next sp, 1sc into next dc, rep from * to end. Turn. 17sc.

9th row 3ch, 2dc into base of 3ch, *1 cluster into next sc, 1dc into each of next 3sc, rep from * to end, finishing with 3dc all into last sc. Turn.

10th row 1ch, 1sc into each dc to end. 21 sc.

11th row 3ch, *1 cluster into next sc, 1dc into each of next 3sc, rep from * to end. Turn.

12th row 1ch, 1sc into each dc to end. Turn.

13th row 4ch, *skip next sc, 1dc into next sc, 1ch, rep from * to end. Turn.

14th row 1ch, *1sc into first dc, 1sc into next sp, rep from * to end. Turn.

15th row 3ch, *skip next sc, 1dc, 2ch and 1dc all into next sc, skip next sc, rep from * to end, finishing with 1dc into last sc. Turn.

16th row 1sc into first dc, 3sc into each sp, 1sc into turning ch. Turn.

17th row As 13th.

18th row As 14th.

Working into back loops only, work 1 row sc without shaping. (Work 1 more row here for 2nd wing.)

Next row 1sc into each of next 19sc, turn.

Next row 1sc into each sc to end. Turn.

Next row 1sc into each of next 16sc, turn.

Next row 1sc into each sc to end. Turn.

Next row 1sc into each of next 14sc, turn.

Next row 1sc into each sc to end. Turn.

Next row 1sc into each of next 11sc, turn.

Next row 1sc into each sc to end. Turn.

Next row 1sc into each of next 7sc.

Work 1 row of sc around outer edge of wing, working over wire at the same time.

Fasten off.

Make another wing in the same way, noting the exception in parentheses. Sew wings and feelers in place, sewing across center of feelers.

Ladybug pillow

The huge ladybug on the next page is not just for decoration; it also makes a comfortable pillow.

Size
Approx 20×18in (50×45cm).

Materials
- 2oz (50g) of a medium-weight mohair in brown
- 3oz (75g) of a knitting worsted in brown (A)
- 6oz (150g) of a knitting worsted in red (B)
- 1oz (25g) of a knitting worsted in beige (C)
- Sizes E and J (3.50 and 6.50mm) crochet hooks
- 1yd (1m) of heavyweight batting Polyester fiberfill

Gauge
19hdc and 13 rows to 4in (10cm) worked on size E (3.50mm) hook with knitting worsted. 18sc and 20 rows to 4in (10cm) worked on size E (3.50mm) hook with knitting worsted. 14hdc and 10 rows to 4in (10cm) worked on size J (6.50mm) hook with mohair.

Body
Under section
Using smaller hook and knitting worsted in A, make 4ch.

Base row 1hdc into 3rd ch from hook, 1hdc into last ch. Turn. 3 sts.

Cont in hdc, inc one hdc at each end of every row until there are 39hdc. Work 1 row, then inc one hdc at each end of next and every foll 3rd row until there are 49hdc.

Now dec one hdc at each end of every other row until 37hdc rem, then at each end of every row until 11hdc rem. Work 4 rows without shaping.

Next row 2ch, work next 3hdc tog, 1 hdc into each of next 3hdc, work next 3 hdc tog, 1hdc into top of 2ch. Turn.

Next row 2ch, work next 2hdc tog, 1hdc into next hdc, work next 2hdc tog, 1hdc into top of 2ch.

Fasten off.

Upper section
Using larger hook and mohair, make 3ch.

Base row 1hdc into last ch. Turn. 2 sts.

Cont in hdc, inc one hdc at each end of every row until there are 30hdc, then at each end of every other row until there are 38hdc. Work 1 row.

Now dec one hdc at each end of every row until 14hdc rem, then at each end of every other row until 8hdc rem. Work 2 rows without shaping.

Next row 2ch, (work next 3hdc tog) twice, 1hdc into top of 2ch. Fasten off.

Wings (make 4)
Using smaller hook and knitting worsted in B, make 3ch.

Base row 1sc into 2nd ch from hook, 1sc into last ch. Turn.

Cont in sc, inc one sc at each end of next and every foll alternate row until there are 17sc, then at each end of every foll 4th row until there are 43sc.

Now dec one sc at each end of every row until 7sc rem. Fasten off.

Join knitting worsted in C to beg of decreases and using smaller hook work 18sc along row ends, 1sc into each of the 7sc and 18sc along row ends to end of decreases, turn.

Next row Sl st over first sc, 1sc into each sc to within last sc, sl st into last sc. Turn.
Next row Skip first sl st, now sl st over first 3sc, 1sc into each sc to within last 4 sc, sl st into next sc. Turn.
Rep last row 4 times more. Fasten off.
Make another piece in the same way.

Spots (make 6)
Using larger hook and mohair, wind yarn twice around finger, remove loop from finger and work 6sc into loop,

sl st into first sc.
Pull loose end of yarn to close hole.
Next round Work 2sc into each sc all around, sl st into first sc. Fasten off.

Feelers (make 2)
Using smaller hook and knitting worsted in A, make 12ch.
Base row 1sc into 2nd ch from hook, 1sc into each ch to end. Turn.
Work 2 rows in sc. Fasten off.
Fold the strip in half lengthwise and join the seam.

To finish
Join body sections tog, leaving an opening for stuffing. Stuff with fiberfill, then slip stitch opening. With RS tog, place 2 wing sections on top of body and sew in place.
Using one of the wing sections as a pattern, cut 2 pieces of batting to shape. Lay batting on top of wing sections on body, then lay second section on top and overcast edges together.
Sew 3 spots to each wing. Sew feelers to head.

Kim Sayer

26

Crochet / COURSE 88

*Broomstick crochet
*Twisting stitches from right to left
*Twisting stitches from left to right
*Broomstick crochet pattern variations
*Pattern for a soft stole

Broomstick crochet

This form of crochet derives its name from the large needle or pin which is used along with an ordinary crochet hook to make the stitches. Although it would be quite simple to make your own pin from a piece of doweling or even a broom handle, it is more usual to use one of the knitting broomstick pins which are available in various sizes. These are very large knitting needles made especially for broomstick crochet or bulky knitting; they have a point at one end and a stopper at the other end which prevents the loops from slipping off the needle.

Unlike ordinary crochet, it is necessary to work a number of loops onto the pin equivalent to the width of the fabric being made—as in knitting—rather than working with one loop only as you would normally do when making a crochet fabric. If you are making a very wide piece, it may be impossible to fit all the loops onto the pin at the same time, and in this case several strips can be made and sewn or crocheted together to make one piece. To make the various patterns, you slip the loops off the pin and then crochet them together to form groups.

Pattern variations are achieved by altering the number of loops worked together at one time, or by twisting the loops either to the right or to the left.
In this course we show you how to work the basic broomstick crochet patterns using a 1in (25mm) pin and size K (7.00mm) hook in conjunction with a bulky knitting yarn, so that you can see exactly how the technique is worked. Once you have mastered the basic method, try using soft mohair to create fabrics ideal for shawls, blankets, scarves and many other crochet items.

Twisting stitches from right to left

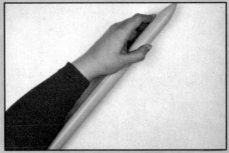

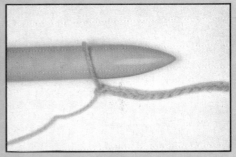

1 Make a length of chains equivalent to the width of the fabric, using the size K (7.00mm) crochet hook. In the pattern shown here 5 loops are to be worked together at a time, so you should make a multiple of five chains.

2 Experiment with the pin before you start working, to see which is the most comfortable way of holding it. You can either tuck the shaft of the pin under your elbow or hold it between your knees.

3 Hold the crochet hook in the normal way and extend the working loop so that you can slip it easily over the end of the pin.

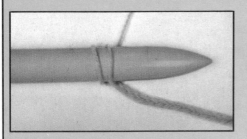

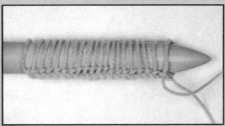

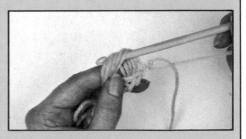

4 Insert the hook through the 2nd chain from the pin, wind the yarn over the hook, draw a loop through the chain and extend it so that it can be slipped over the pin.

5 Continue to draw loops through each chain to the end, slipping each loop over and onto the pin until all the chains have been worked in this way. To prevent a taut edge do not pull the loops tightly over the pin.

6 Slip all the loops off the pin as shown here. Hold the loops in the left hand and insert the hook from right to left through the first 5 loops.

continued

Mike Berend

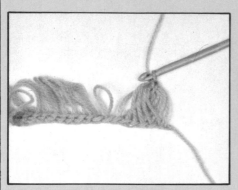

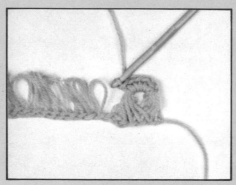

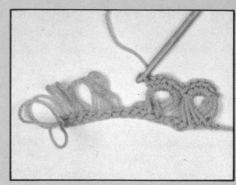

7 Wind the yarn around the hook. Draw a loop through the center of the 5-loop group and make one chain.

8 Now work 5 single crochets through the center of the loops, thus twisting the loops from right to left and completing the first group.

9 Insert the hook from right to left through the next 5 loops as before and work 5 single crochets into the center of this group to make the 2nd group.

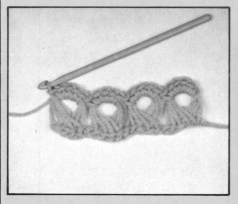

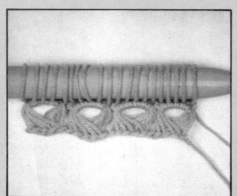

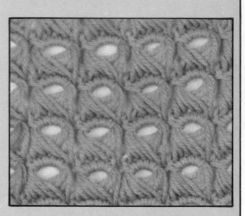

10 Continue to work 5 loops together in this way across the row to complete the first pattern repeat.

11 To continue working the pattern, do not turn the work but extend the working loop over the pin, skip the first single crochet then draw a loop through each single crochet made in the previous row. Make sure that you have the same number of loops as before.

12 Do not turn the work but slip all the loops off the hook. Complete the 2nd single crochet row in exactly the same way as before, working steps 7 to 10 once more. To make a complete fabric, repeat the loop and single crochet rows each time in exactly the same way throughout.

Twisting stitches from left to right

To change the appearance of the basic 5-loop pattern, you twist the loops from left to right instead of from right to left. Work the loops onto the pin in exactly the same way as when working the loops from right to left, using a 1in (25mm) pin and size K(7.00mm) hook.

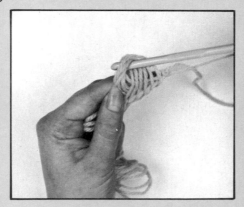

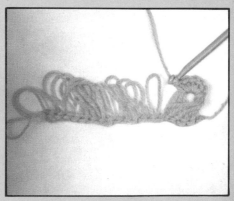

1 Slip all the loops off the hook and insert the hook through the first 5 loops, taking it through the loops from left to right as shown here.

2 Wind yarn over hook and draw through a loop then make one chain to hold the loops in place. Now work 5 single crochets into the center of these loops to complete the first group.

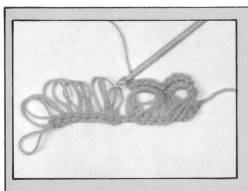

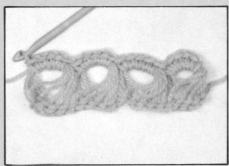

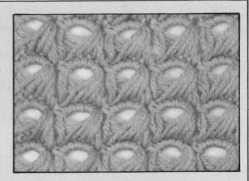

3 Insert the hook from left to right through the next 5 loops and work 5 single crochets into the center of this group, thus twisting the loops from left to right.

4 Continue to work 5-loop groups in the same way across the chains to complete the first loop row.

5 To complete the pattern, alternate loop rows and single crochet rows following the instructions for twisting loops from right to left, but inserting the hook through the loops from left to right each time instead of from right to left. If you are working more single crochet rows between the loop rows, remember to turn the work at end of single crochet rows.

Broomstick crochet pattern variations

It is easy to change the appearance of the basic broomstick crochet pattern. One method is to alter the number of loops worked together at a time—here we show samples in which three, four and five loops have been twisted—and to change the direction in which the loops are twisted. A variety of effects can also be achieved with different yarn, and here we have worked samples in worsted, bulky and mohair yarns to show the range of textures that can be achieved.

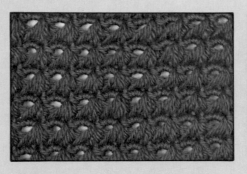

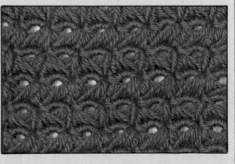

1 Using knitting worsted, make a number of chains divisible by 3 and follow the instructions for working loops from right to left. On single crochet rows work 3 single crochets instead of 5 into the center of each 3-loop group so that you maintain the correct number of stitches each time.

2 In this sample—again in knitting worsted—4 loops have been worked together on each loop row, with 4 single crochets worked into the center of each group. Alternate the loop and single crochet rows as before but twist the loops first from left to right on the first single crochet row and then from the right to the left on the 2nd single crochet row alternately up the fabric.

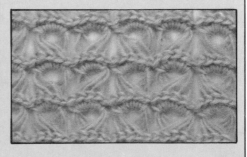

3 Here we have made the same sample using a bulky yarn and a larger pin and hook to create a bulkier fabric. We have used the ridged side as the right side as on the stole on page 31.

4 In this sample 5 loops have been twisted first from left to right and then from right to left alternately across each row. Thus the first group is worked from left to right and the 2nd from right to left, and so on across the row. Work each single crochet row in the same way.

5 The same sample has here been worked in a soft, brushed yarn using a larger hook and pin for a light, lacy look. Again, the ridged side is the right side.

Mike Berend

Soft stole

This broomstick wrapover can either be worn belted, like a loose, open-sided tunic, or as an ordinary shawl or scarf.

Size
Width across back, 33½in.
Length, 30¾in.

Materials
14oz (400g) of a medium weight mohair
Size K (8.00mm) crochet hook
1in (25mm) knitting needle

Gauge
6 groups of loops to 4in (10cm) on size K (8.00mm) hook.

Right front
Using size K (8.00mm) hook, chain 50.
Base row Transfer loop on hook to the needle, skip first ch, *insert hook into next ch, yo and draw through a loop, transfer loop onto needle, rep from * to last ch. 50 loops.
1st row Insert hook from right to left into first 2 loops and remove them from needles, 1ch, 2sc into loops, *insert hook from right to left into next 2 loops and remove them from needle, 2sc into loops, rep from * to end. 25 groups.
2nd row Transfer loop on hook to needle, skip first sc at base of transferred loop, insert hook into *back loop only* of next sc, yo and draw through a loop, transfer loop to needle, rep from * to end. 50 loops.
First and 2nd rows form patt.
Cont in patt until 20 rows of loops have

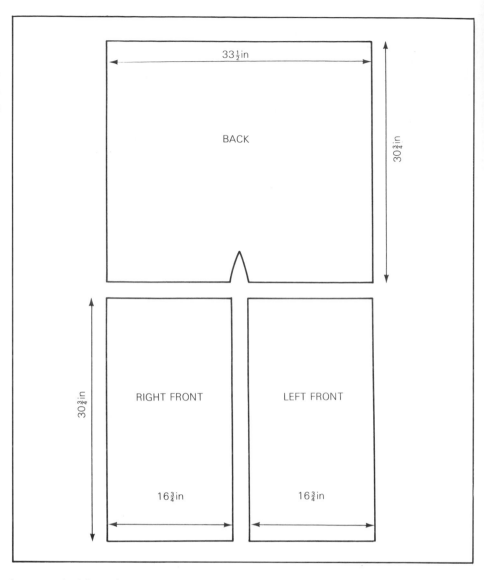

been worked from beg.
Work first row once more.
Fasten off.

Left front
Work as given for right front.

Back
Using size K (8.00mm) hook, chain 100.
Work base row as given for right front. 100 loops.
Cont in patt as for right front until 17 rows of loops have been worked from beg.
Work first row once more.
Divide for neck
Next row Transfer loop on hook to needle, skip first sc at base of transferred loop, *insert hook into *back loop only* of next sc, yo and draw through a loop, transfer loop to needle, rep from * across first 50 sts. 25 groups.
Work patt twice more.
Work first row once more.
Fasten off.
Return to skipped sc at beg of neck shaping and rejoin yarn to next sc.
Work 2nd side of neck to match first.

To finish
Do not press.
Seam fronts to back with sc.

*More simple toy shapes
*Adding features to toys
*Hair for toys
*Pattern for a knitted doll

More simple toy shapes

Many different kinds of knitted toys can be made by combining simple shapes—rectangles, circles and squares—in various ways. The resulting knitted shape is then gathered and stuffed.

Toys do not have to be rigid; they can be made with movable limbs (see the doll on page 36).
Here we show a simple toy shape, knitted in two pieces and then stuffed and sewn,

and a doll knitted in several pieces, stuffed and sewn together so that the arms and legs can be moved.
From these two simple figures many different toys can be made.

1 For a simple toy shape, using No. 6 (4½mm) needles and knitting worsted, cast on 18 stitches for lower edge. Work in stockinette stitch for 4in (10cm) for body.

2 Cast on 12 stitches at beginning of next 2 rows for arms. Continue in stockinette stitch for a further 1¼in (3cm). Now bind off 12 stitches at beginning of next 2 rows. This completes the arms.

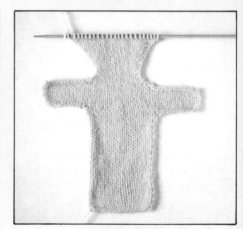

3 Shape for the head by decreasing one stitch at each end of next 3 rows, then increasing one stitch at each end of every other row until there are 24 stitches.

4 Continue without shaping for 1¼in (3cm). Now decrease one stitch at each end of every row until 12 stitches remain. Bind off.

5 Make another piece in the same way. With RS of both pieces facing, sew around outer edge, leaving lower edge open for stuffing. Turn knitting right side out.

6 Stuff firmly with foam chips, fiberfill, scraps of yarn or old pantyhose, then slip stitch along the opening. Complete toy by working backstitch through all thicknesses for 2¾in (7cm) to denote legs and adding features to face.

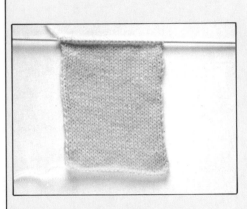

7 For jointed doll, using No. 6 (4½mm) needles and knitting worsted, cast on 26 stitches for lower edge of body. Work in stockinette stitch for 4¼in (11cm).

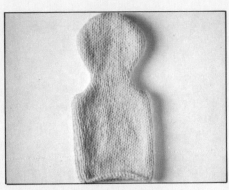

8 Bind off 2 stitches at beginning of next 4 rows for shoulders. Now shape head and finish, following steps 3 to 5. Stuff firmly and slip stitch along opening.

9 Using same yarn and needles, cast on 26 stitches. Work in stockinette stitch for 6in (15cm) for leg. Cut off yarn leaving a long end, thread end through remaining stitches, gather tightly and secure.

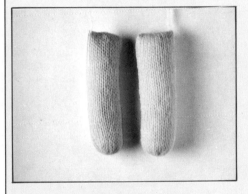

10 Fold knitting in half, with RS together, and join seam. Turn knitting right side out. Stuff firmly; slip stitch opening. Repeat.

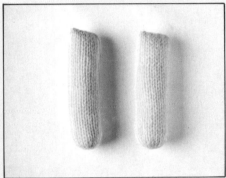

11 For arms cast on 20 sts and work in stockinette stitch for 4¾in (12cm). Finish each piece as for legs.

12 Overcast straight edge of arms and legs to body, then complete with features.

Adding features to toys

Features play a very important part in toy making. The entire look of a doll or animal is determined by the expression on its face and the finishing touches on the body.

Here we show some features made from felt and others worked in embroidery. Felt can be cut into many interesting shapes and either glued or sewn to the knitted sections to form amusing expres-

sions. There are many different embroidery stitches that can be used to form features. Here we show the basic stitches that can be used, though others could be equally effective.

Felt features

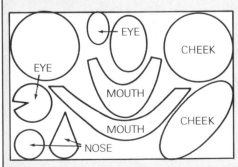

1 Here is a selection of eyes, noses, cheeks and mouths that can be traced and used as patterns for felt.

2 Choose your shapes, then, using tracing paper and a pencil, trace the shape. Cut out the shape and use this as your pattern. Pin the pattern on the felt, then cut out the felt shape.

3 Arrange the features on the face, and glue the features in position with fabric glue.

continued

4 The features can be sewn in place using matching thread. Pin the features to the knitting, then overcast around the edge of each piece.

5 You can see that by using different shapes you can achieve many different looks. This doll has a very sad face.

6 To make this pig's face, use the same shaped head but cut out a set of different features.

Embroidered features

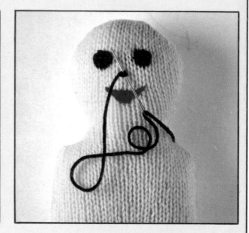

1 Begin by outlining the main features in backstitch. Here the shapes for the eyes and mouth have been outlined.

2 Now the area is filled in using straight stitches and working vertically across the shape. Do not pull the stitches too tightly; this will distort the shape. This stitch is called satin stitch.

3 The pupils and nostrils can be formed by working French knots. Insert the needle from back to front in the appropriate position. Wind the yarn clockwise once around the needle.

4 Holding the yarn firmly, insert needle close to the point at which the yarn first emerged and pull the thread quickly through the loop or loops. For a larger knot, use a thicker yarn.

5 To finish the nose, work a few back stitches around the French knots to form the shape as shown.

6 This cat's face uses the same stitches to form eyes, nose, mouth and whiskers.

Hair for toys

Hair can be made from strands of yarn combined in a variety of ways, some of which we show here. If you want the toy's hair to resemble human hair, copy the way real hair grows, from a crown or a part, and use yarns that suggests the colors and textures of hair—for example bouclé yarn gives a curly look. There is, of course, no need for the toy's hair to look realistic—have fun making "hair" in fantastic colors and textures to amuse a child.

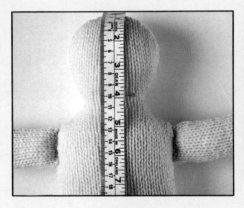

1 Measure from top of head for length of hair required, then from front of head to nape of neck. Cut a piece of cardboard using these measurements.

2 Wind yarn for hair around the cardboard, filling the width of the cardboard completely.

3 Backstitch the yarn across one short end of the cardboard to hold the strands together. Cut across the other short end and remove yarn from cardboard.

4 Place seam in the center of the head, then sew hair to back of head along seam. Tie hair into bunches at side of head. Trim the ends.

5 For braided hair, follow steps 1 to 3, allowing three times the length needed for each braid when measuring. Place seam at center of head, then sew hair to head along seam.

6 Divide one side of hair into three equal groups, then braid hair by taking right-hand group over center group, then left-hand group over center group alternately to end of strands. Secure with a bow. Trim the ends.

7 For short hair, cut yarn into equal lengths. Tie a strand of yarn around the center and, using this as the crown, sew to head. Arrange strands around head and tack some strands to head to keep them in place. Trim the ends.

8 For a mane or very short hair, a knotted fringe can be worked on the head. Cut yarn into equal lengths. Using a crochet hook, insert hook through one stitch, fold one strand of yarn in half, place the loop on the hook and draw the hook through the fabric, drawing the loop through. Now draw the ends of the yarn through the loop on hook. Continue to knot hair over head.

Fred Mancini

Knitted doll

Make friends with our pretty doll. She's easy to knit and is sure to delight her small owner.

Michael Boys

Size
Height, approx 27in (68cm).

Materials
9oz (250g) of a sport yarn in green
5oz (125g) in flesh color
4oz (100g) in white
1oz (25g) in black
1oz (25g) in rust
1lb (400g) of polyester fiberfill
1yd (1m) of 1in (2.5cm)-wide ribbon
Felt for features
3 buttons
1¾yd (1.5m) of round elastic
1 pair No. 3 (3¼mm) knitting needles
Medium-size crochet hook

Body and head
Using No. 3 (3¼mm) needles and flesh color, cast on 33 sts. Beg with a K row, cont in stockinette st inc one st at beg of next 4 rows. 37 sts. Work 58 rows straight. Bind off 6 sts at beg of next 2 rows. 25 sts. Dec one st at each end of next row. 23 sts. Inc one st at each end of next 3 rows. 29 sts. Inc one st at beg of next 8 rows. 37 sts. Work 38 rows straight. Dec one st at each end of next 9 rows. 19 sts. Bind off. Make another piece in same way.

Arms (make 2)
Using No. 3 (3¼mm) needles and flesh color, cast on 11 sts. Beg with a K row, cont in stockinette st inc one st at beg of next 6 rows. 17 sts. Work 6 rows straight. Dec one st at beg of next 4 rows. 13 sts. Work 1 row, so ending with a K row. Cut off yarn and leave sts on a spare needle. Make another piece in the same way, but do not cut off yarn.
Next row P to end, then onto same needle P the sts of first piece. 26 sts. Work 8 rows.
Next row K1, insert tip of left-hand needle from front to back under strand between 2 needles and K into back of new loop— called pick up and K or puk; K to last st, puk, K1. 28 sts. Work 9 rows.
Next row K1, puk, K to last st, puk, K1. 30 sts.
Work 40 rows straight. Dec one st at each end of next 14 rows. Cut off yarn, leaving a long end. Thread end through rem sts, gather tightly and secure.

Legs (make 2)
Using No. 3 (3¼mm) needles and flesh color, cast on 18 sts. Beg with a K row, cont in stockinette st inc one st at beg of next 4 rows. 22 sts. Work 4 rows. Dec one st at beg of next row and at this same edge on foll 7 rows. 14 sts. Work 1 row, so ending with a K row. Cut off yarn and leave sts on a holder. Using No. 3 (3¼mm) needles and flesh color, cast on 18 sts. Beg with a K row, cont in stockinette st inc one st at beg of next 4 rows. 22 sts. Work 4 rows. Dec one st at end of next

row and at this same edge on foll 7 rows. 14 sts. Work 1 row, so ending with a K row.
Next row P to end, then onto same needle P the sts of first piece. 28 sts. Work 8 rows.
Next row K1, puk, K to last st, puk, K1. 30 sts.
Work 9 rows.
Next row K1, puk, K to last st, puk, K1. 32 sts.
Work 60 rows. Bind off.

To finish
With RS of both pieces of body tog, sew around edge, leaving opening for stuffing.
Turn doll RS out. Stuff body, then slip stitch opening. Join seams of arms and legs, leaving top edge open. Stuff arms and legs, then slip stitch opening. Work 4 lines of backstitch along each hand to indicate fingers. Sew arms and legs in place. Cut features from felt, then glue or sew to face.
Make braids in rust foll instructions on page 35. Tie ribbon in a bow around the end of each braid.

Dress
Using No. 3 (3¼mm) needles and green cast on 149 sts. K 3 rows. With green K1 row and P1 row. Join on white. Beg patt.
1st row K2 green, 1 white, (3 green, 1 white) to last 2 sts, 2 green.
2nd row P with green.
3rd row K with green.
4th row P1 white, (3 green, 1 white) to end.
5th row K with green.
6th row P with green.
These 6 rows form patt. Rep them 8 times more, then work first row again.
Dec row P2, (P2 tog, P1) 49 times. 100 sts.
Cut off yarn.
Divide for yoke
With RS facing, place first 25 sts on a holder, rejoin yarn to next st, K49 for front, turn and leave rem 25 sts on a holder.
Beg with a 4th row, patt 17 rows.
Cast on 22 sts at beg of next 2 rows for sleeves. 93 sts. Working 22 sts of each sleeve in green only, cont in patt on center 49 sts, work 30 rows. Bind off.
With RS facing, rejoin yarn to first set of 25 sts and K to end of row. Cont in green only, work 18 rows. Cast on 22 sts at beg of next row for sleeve. 47 sts. Work 30 rows. Bind off.
With RS facing, rejoin yarn to rem sts and work as first side, but work 17 rows before casting on sts for sleeve.

Pocket
Using No. 3 (3¼mm) needles and white, cast on 8 sts. Work 1 row, then inc one st at beg of next 4 rows. 12 sts. Work 8 rows. Bind off.

To finish
Join back seam of skirt to beg of yoke. Join underarm seams and yoke and shoulder seams to fit neck of doll. Using crochet hook and green, work a row of single crochet evenly along back opening and edge of each sleeve.
Work 3 button loops on right side of back opening.

Collar
Using No. 3 (3¼mm) needles and white, cast on 30 sts. K8 rows. Bind off. Make another piece in same way. Sew on buttons. Sew on collar and pocket as shown.

Bloomers
Using Using No. 3 (3¼mm) needles and white, cast on 58 sts. K2 rows. Cut off white, join on green. Beg with a P row, work 48 rows stockinette st, so ending with a K row. Cut off yarn and leave sts on a spare needle. Work another piece in same way, but do not cut off yarn.
Next row P to end, then onto same needle P the sts of first piece. 116 sts. Work 34 rows stockinette st, then work 3 rows K1, P1 ribbing. Bind off in ribbing.
Join center back seam and inner leg seam. Thread elastic through WS of knitting, 7 rows from cast-on edge, to gather.

Cap
Using No. 3 (3¼mm) needles and green, cast on 150 sts for brim. K 2 rows. Cut off green. Join on white. K 6 rows.
Dec row (K1, K2 tog) to end. 100 sts. Work 5 rows stockinette st. Cut off yarn and leave sts on a spare needle.
Using No. 3 (3¼mm) needles and white, cast on 22 sts for crown. Beg with a K row, cont in stockinette st inc one st at each end of next 14 rows. 50 sts. Now inc one st at beg of next 22 rows. 72 sts. Work 15 rows straight. Dec one st at beg of next 22 rows. 50 sts. Now dec one st at each end of next 14 rows. Bind off. With RS facing, using No. 3 (3¼mm) needles and white, pick up and K 100 sts evenly around edge of crown. With RS of brim and crown tog, K 1 row, working into sts on crown and corresponding sts on brim. Bind off.
Thread elastic through back of sts around joining, gather tightly to fit head. Join row ends of brim.

Shoes (make 2)
Using No. 3 (3¼mm) needles and black, cast on 22 sts. Beg with a K row, cont in stockinette st inc one st at beg of next 4 rows. 26 sts. Work 6 rows. Dec one st at beg of next row and at this same edge on foll 7 rows. 18 sts. Bind off. Make another piece, reversing shaping. Join back and toe seam.
Make a button loop to simulate fastening.

Shoestring

Sensational sequins

To jazz up a plain cardigan or pullover for evening wear, add some sequin motifs. These are available from notions counters, craft stores, and specialist bead shops.

Materials
Plain sweater
One or more sequin motifs
Matching thread

1 Try on the sweater. If it is a cardigan, fasten it as you plan to wear it. Pin the motifs in the desired position; adjust them if necessary until you are pleased with the effect.

2 Remove the sweater. Add a few more pins to hold the motifs in place quite securely.
3 Using a double strand of thread, sew the motif in place, working around the edges through the backing. Take care not to pull or pucker the knitting.
4 If desired, matching braid can be used to trim the front or lower edges of a cardigan.

Knitting / COURSE 84

*Padded features on toys
*Pompom toys
*Pattern for a white rabbit

Padded features on toys

As shown on pages 33 and 34, toys can be made to look distinctive by changing their features, and the effective use of padding can make features look even more individual and appealing.

Use padding to give a three-dimensional effect to prominent features such as the cheeks of the rabbit shown below. Padding can also strengthen features like hands, ears and feet which are likely to be grasped by small hands.

There are two methods of adding padding to features. In the first method a single layer of felt is sewn to the knitting and the padding is inserted as you sew—the padded cheeks on the clown below are made this way.

The second method involves two pieces of felt which are sewn together leaving a small opening. The padding is then inserted, the opening is sewn together neatly and finally the feature is sewn to the toy. We have used this method for the duck's beak below.

Small amounts of fiberfill are ideal for stuffing since they mold well and are easily compressed. Remember to insert enough padding into a feature like a nose or tail to make it firm and rounded. If too little padding is used, the feature will not hold its shape; in fact it is a good idea to over-pad slightly since the filling settles with time.

Fred Mancini

This rabbit has padded cheeks. The cheeks should be cut into shape and the small felt pieces and embroidery added before the cheeks are sewn to the face and padded.

This clown has padded cheeks, nose and hands. Cut circles of felt for cheeks and nose. Pad the cheeks while sewing them to the face. Gather the edge of circle for nose, pad firmly, then sew it to face. Cut hand shapes from felt—two pieces for each hand. Join edges, leaving an opening for padding. Insert padding, then join the opening. Then sew hands to arms.

This duck hand puppet has a padded beak. Cut the beak shape from felt, cutting two pieces. Join the edges, leaving an opening for padding. Insert padding, then join the opening and sew the beak in position along the top edge, leaving the bottom loose.

Pompom toys

Toys can be formed by making and joining pompoms of different sizes (see Volume 6, page 46, for making a pompom). Sections can be worked in different colors to form features. The pompoms can also be trimmed into various shapes to form noses, legs and tails.

Here we show a selection of toys made with pompoms, showing the effect of using more than one color and some of the shapes that can be achieved by trimming.

For dog make pompoms in white as follows:
Body 2 × 2¼in (6cm)-diameter pompoms.
Head 1 × 2¼in (6cm)-diameter pompoms.
Legs 4 × 1¼in (3cm)-diameter pompoms.

Tail 1 × 1¼in (3cm)-diameter pompom. Sew all pompoms together, shape head, legs and tail and complete with felt features as shown.

For gnome make pompoms as follows:
Body 1 × 3¼in (8cm)-diameter pompom, two-thirds worked in green, the other third worked in white.
Head 1 × 2¼in (6cm)-diameter pompom, two-thirds worked in green, the other third worked in flesh color.
Beard 1 × 1¼in (3cm)-diameter pompom, worked in white.
Hat 1 × 1½in (4cm)-diameter pompom, three-quarters worked in green, the other quarter worked in white.
Sew all pompoms together, shape beard and hat and complete with felt features as shown.

For penguin make pompoms as follows:
Body 1 × 3¼in (8cm)-diameter pompom, one half worked in white, the other half worked in black.
Head 1 × 2¼in (6cm)-diameter pompom, worked in black with 2 small sections worked in white for eyes.
Nose 1 × 1¼in (3cm)-diameter pompom, worked in white.
Sew all pompoms together, and finish with felt features as shown.

For wasp make pompoms as follows:
Body 1 × 3¼in (8cm)-diameter pompom, alternating rounds of yellow and black.
Head 1 × 2¼in (6cm)-diameter pompom, worked in black.
Sew pompoms together and complete with felt features as shown.

White rabbit

If you go down to the woods today . . . you'll meet our white rabbit. He's just the sort of cuddly friend that "children" of all ages love.

Size
Height, approx 30in (76cm).

Materials
8oz (200g) of a knitting worsted
    in white
5oz (125g) in blue
1oz (25g) in red
13×18in (31×46cm) gray felt
9×13in (23×31cm) pink felt
Scraps of black, blue and white
    felt for features
Matching thread
2 blue buttons
Polyester fiberfill
1 pair No. 3 (3¼mm) knitting needles
Medium-size crochet hook

Back first leg
Using No. 3 (3¼mm) needles and white, cast on 36 sts for sole of foot.
Working in stockinette st throughout, inc one st at beg of next 8 rows. 44 sts. Work 11 rows without shaping. Dec one st at beg of next row and at this same edge on foll 9 rows. 34 sts. Now dec two sts at beg of next row and at this same edge on foll 3 rows. 26 sts.
Work 1 row.
Cut off white.
Join on blue.
Inc one st at end of every other row until there are 38 sts; end with a P row.
Cut off yarn and leave sts on a spare needle.

Back second leg
As first leg, reversing shaping; do not cut off yarn.
Next row K to end, then onto same needle K the sts of first leg. 76 sts.
Work 3 rows. Inc one st at each end of next and foll 4th rows. 80 sts.
Work 24 rows without shaping. Now dec one st at each end of next and every foll 6th row until 72 sts rem. Work 5 rows. Cut off blue. Join on white.
Work 4 rows. Dec one st at each end of next and foll 4th-row. 68 sts. Work 4 rows.
Cast on 20 sts at beg of next 2 rows for arms. 108 sts. Inc one st at beg of next 8 rows. 116 sts. Work 14 rows without shaping. Dec one st at beg of next 8 rows, 108 sts. Bind off 28 sts at beg of next 2 rows. 52 sts. This completes the arms. Dec one st at each end of next 4 rows. 44 sts. Work 1 row. Inc one st at each end of next 12 rows. 68 sts. Work 15 rows without shaping. Dec one st at each end of next and every foll 3rd row until 50 sts rem, then at beg of every row until 40 sts rem. Work 8 rows. Dec one st at each end of next 9 rows. 22 sts. Bind off.

Front
Work as given for back.

Suspenders (make 2)
Using No. 3 (3¼mm) needles and blue, cast on 12 sts. Work in stockinette st for 18½in (47cm) or required length. Bind off.

Bow tie
Using No. 3 (3¼mm) needles and red, cast on 12 sts. Work in stockinette st for 8¾in (22cm). Bind off.
Using crochet hook and red, make a ch 22in (56cm) long. Fasten off.

To finish
With RS of both pieces facing, sew around edges, leaving an opening for stuffing. Turn RS out. Stuff firmly, then slip stitch opening. Sew suspenders in position on back, cross them at back, fasten at front with buttons. Join short ends of bow tie, then fold in half. Tie crochet chain around center of tie to gather, then tie chain around neck. Using trace pattern cut cheeks and outer ears from gray felt. Cut inner ears from pink felt. Cut eyelids and nose from black felt. Cut pupils from blue felt and eyes and teeth from white felt. Sew pupils, eyelids and nose onto cheeks. Embroider features on face as indicated, working French knots, backstitch and long straight stitches.
Position felt on face, then using matching thread sew all around edge, stuffing cheeks with fiberfill. Sew inner ears to outer ears, then sew ears in position, Using white, make a pompom for tail. Sew tail to back.

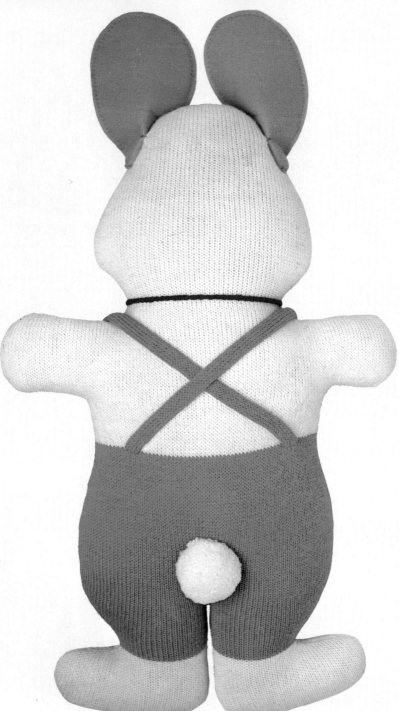

Simon Butcher

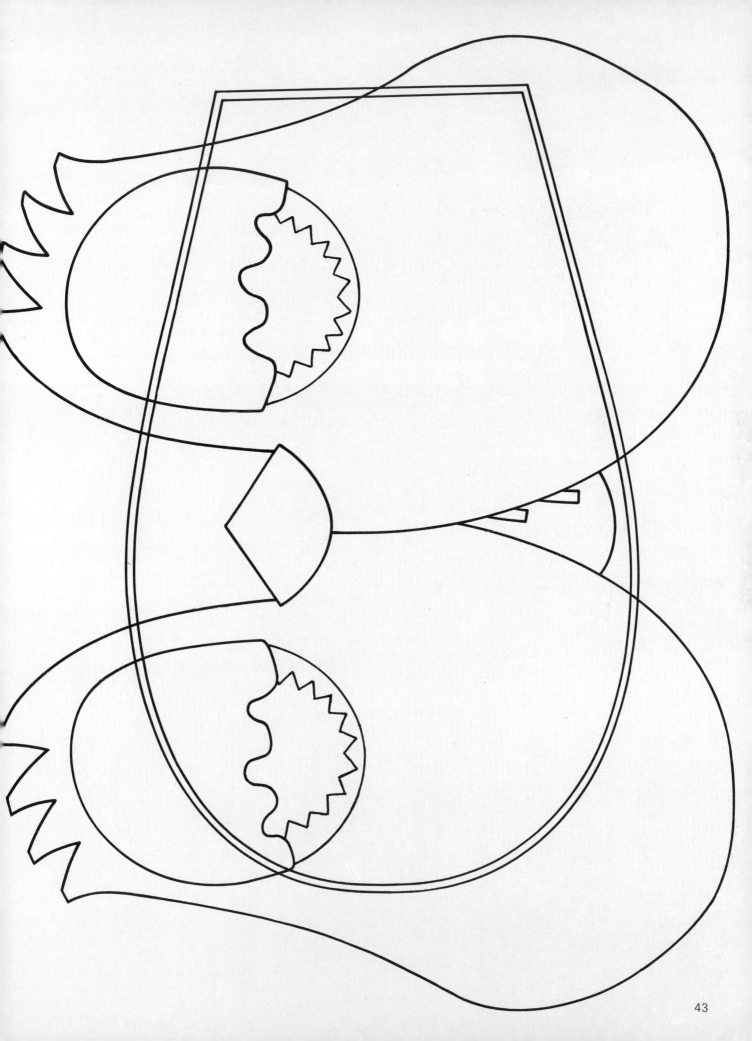

*Double decreasing
*Decreasing slanting to the left
*Decreasing slanting to the right
*Vertical double decrease
*Stitch Wise: Lace patterns
*Pattern for a woman's tunic-style sweater

Double decreasing

A double decrease reduces three stitches to one, often in a decorative way. It is commonly used in chevron patterns, at the point of a V neckline or in openwork and lace patterns (see Stitch Wise on page 46). Worked across the entire fabric, double decreases can also be used to produce a diagonal mock seam between rows running at right angles to each other, as in the tunic on page 47. The simplest way of double decreasing is to knit three stitches together. Another way, which creates a more attractive finish, is to use two single decreases together, pairing them to right and left. In this course we introduce a third method, which involves decreasing two stitches in various ways so that the decrease appears to be mitered. The top stitch can slope either to the right or to the left; or it can run vertically.

Decrease slanting to the left

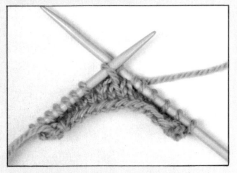

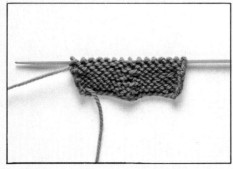

1 This decrease is worked on alternate right-side rows only in the center of the fabric—not at the sides. Knit to the center 3 stitches, slip the next stitch; knit the next 2 stitches together, then pass the slipped stitch over.

2 All wrong-side rows are simply purled. There is little sign of the decrease on the back of the work, except that after a few rows the lines of stitches slope downward from each side toward the center.

3 A succession of decreases should be in line, as shown here, on the right side. Here the slipped stitch is the top one and makes the angle of the decrease; it lies across to the left, making a distinctive pattern.

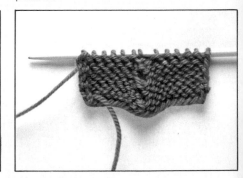

4 It may be necessary to decrease on wrong-side rows instead of on the right side. This method produces the same left-slanting stitch as in the sample in step 3. To work the decrease purl 2 stitches together to form the axis; then replace the resulting stitch on the left-hand needle.

5 Complete the double decrease by inserting the right-hand needle point through the second stitch on the left-hand needle and lifting this stitch over the first (decreased stitch) and off the needle.

6 Now return the original decreased stitch to the right-hand needle and work to the end of the row. All the right side rows must be knitted.

Decrease slanting to the right

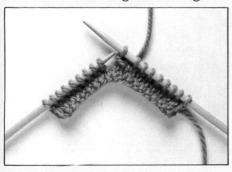 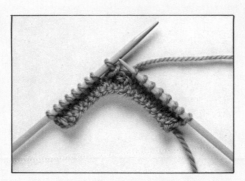 

1 To make a double decrease that slopes to the right, knit to the center 3 stitches. Slip the next stitch knitwise and knit the following stitch. Pass the slipped stitch over the knitted one.

2 Place the knitted stitch on the left-hand needle and lift the next stitch over it and off the needle. Return the knitted stitch to the right-hand needle. The decrease is now complete.

3 Work this type of decrease on alternate rows—simply purling the wrong-side rows—to make this vertical line of successive decreases where the stitch that is passed over the knitted one on the left-hand needle makes a pronounced line slanting to the right.

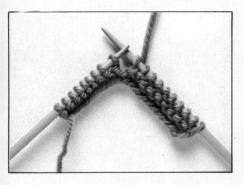  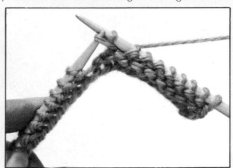

4 If you have to decrease on a wrong-side row, slip the first stitch of the decrease group purlwise. Take the yarn to the back of the work and knit the next stitch, then turn the next stitch on the left-hand needle so that it is twisted.

5 Now put the knitted stitch on the left-hand needle and pass the twisted stitch over it.

6 Replace the knitted stitch on the right-hand needle and lift the slipped stitch over it. The double decrease is now complete. On the right side of the work the decreases slant to the right and resemble the pattern shown in step 3.

Vertical double decrease

 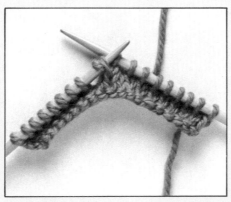 

1 Here the decreasing is worked on RS rows only. Knit to the center 3 stitches in the fabric. Insert right-hand needle into next 2 stitches on left-hand needle as if to knit them together, but simply slip them onto right-hand needle.

2 Knit the next stitch (third one of the group), then lift the 2 slipped stitches over the knitted one. The decrease is now complete.

3 A series of this type of decrease makes a neat vertical line of unbroken chains running up the center of the fabric.

Fred Mancini

Stitch Wise

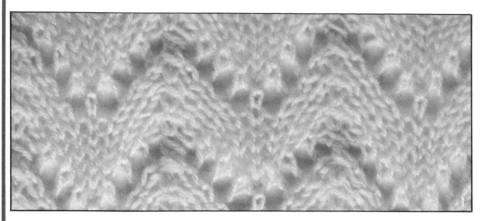

Horseshoe pattern

Cast on a multiple of 10 sts plus 1 extra.
1st row (RS) K1, *yo, K3, sl 1, K2 tog, psso, K3, yo, K1, rep from * to end.
2nd and every other row P to end.
3rd row K1, *K1, yo, K2, sl 1, K2 tog, psso, K2, yo, K2, rep from * to end.
5th row K1, *K2, yo, K1, sl 1, K2 tog, psso, K1, yo, K3, rep from * to end.
7th row K1, *K3, yo, sl 1, K2 tog, psso, yo, K4, rep from * to end.
8th row P to end.
These 8 rows form patt. Rep them throughout.

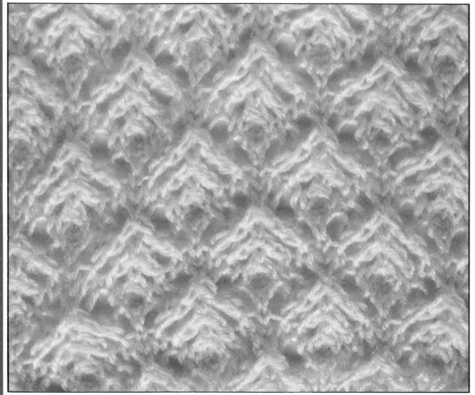

Traditional lace

Cast on a multiple of 8 sts plus 3 extra.
1st row (WS) P to end.
2nd row K4, *yo, sl 1, K2 tog, psso, yo, K5, rep from * ending with K4 instead of K5.
3rd row P3, *yo, P2 tog, P1, P2 tog tbl, yo, P3, rep from * to end.
4th row K2, *yo, sl 1, K1, psso, yo, sl 1, K2 tog, psso, yo, K2 tog, yo, K1, rep from * to last st, K1.
5th row As 3rd.
6th row As 2nd.
7th row As first.
8th row K1, K2 tog, *yo, K5, yo, sl 1, K2 tog, psso, rep from * ending with yo, K5, yo, sl 1, K1, psso, K1.
9th row P2, *P2 tog tbl, yo, P3, yo, P2 tog, P1, rep from * to last st, P1.
10th row K1, K2 tog, *yo, K2 tog, yo, K1, yo, sl 1, K1, psso, yo, sl 1, K2 tog, psso, rep from * ending with yo, K2 tog, yo, K1, (yo, sl 1, K1, psso) twice, K1.
11th row As 9th.
12th row As 8th.
These 12 rows form patt. Rep them throughout.

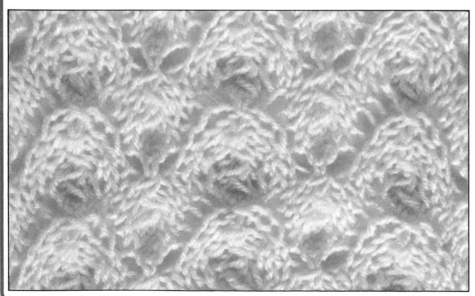

Strawberry motif lace

Cast on a multiple of 12 sts plus 1 extra.
1st row (RS) Sl 1, K1, psso, *K4, yo, K1, yo, K4, sl 1, K2 tog, psso, rep from * ending with sl 1, K1, psso.
2nd row P2 tog, *(P3, yo) twice, P3, P3 tog, rep from * ending with P2 tog.
3rd row Sl 1, K1, psso, *K2, yo, K5, yo, K2, sl 1, K2 tog, psso, rep from * ending with sl 1, K1, psso.
4th row P2 tog, *P1, yo, P7, yo, P1, P3 tog, rep from * ending with P2 tog.
5th row Sl 1, K1, psso, *yo, K9, yo, sl 1, K2 tog, psso, rep from * ending with sl 1, K1, psso.
5th row P1, *yo, P4, P3 tog, P4, yo, P1, rep from * to end.
7th row K2, *yo, K3, sl 1, K2 tog, psso, K3, yo, K3, rep from * ending with K2.
8th row P3, *yo, P2, P3 tog, P2, yo, P5, rep from * ending with P3.

Tunic-style sweater

Bold geometric lines and contrasting colors make a tunic to
add impact to your wardrobe.

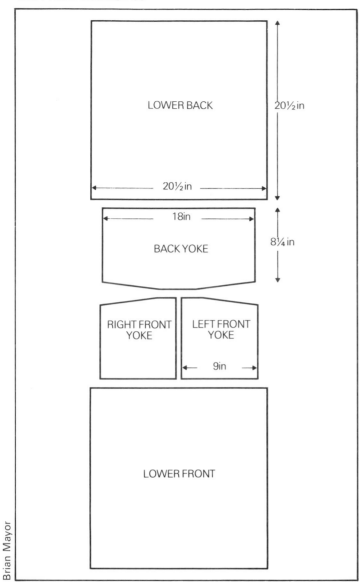

Brian Mayor

Size
To fit 33-37in (84-94cm) bust.
Length, 28¾in (72.5cm).

Materials
*8oz (200g) of a sport yarn in first
color (A)*
6oz (150g) in second color (B)
*4oz (100g) in each of third and
fourth colors (C and D)*
*1 pair each of Nos. 2 and 3 (2¾ and
3¼mm) knitting needles*
1 button

Gauge
26 sts and 40 rows to 4in (10cm) in garter
st on No. 3 (3¼mm) needles.

Lower back
Using No. 3 (3¼mm) needles and D, cast
on 269 sts. Place a marker in center st.
1st row K to end.
2nd row K to one st before center st,
sl 1, K2 tog, psso, K to end.
Rep these 2 rows 3 times more. Cut off D.
Cont in same way, dec at center of

alternate rows, and work in stripe
sequence of 24 rows A, 40 rows C, 62
rows B, 62 rows D, 40 rows A, 24 rows C
and 7 rows B.
Last row Sl 1, K2 tog, psso.
Fasten off.

Lower front
Work as for lower back.

Back yoke
Using No. 3 (3¼mm) needles and A, cast on
116 sts. Work 8¼in (21cm) garter st; end
with a RS row.
Shape shoulders
Bind off 8 sts at beg of next 8 rows.
Leave rem 52 sts on a holder.

Left front yoke
Using No. 3 (3¼mm) needles and A, cast on
58 sts. Work 8¼in (21cm) in garter st;
end with a WS row.
Shape shoulder
Bind off 8 sts at beg of next and foll 3
alternate rows; end at front edge. Leave
rem 26 sts on a holder.

Right front yoke
Work as for left front yoke, reversing
shaping.

Collar
Join shoulder seams. Using No. 2
(2¾mm) needles, B and with WS facing,
K across sts of left front, back neck and
right front. 104 sts.
Work 2¼in (6cm) garter st.
Bind off.

Armhole borders
Using No. 2 (2¾mm) needles, B and with
RS of work facing, pick up and K 106 sts
around armhole. Work 1⅛in (3cm) garter
st; end with a RS row. Bind off.

To finish
Do not press.
Sew yokes to top of lower back and
lower front.
Join side seams, leaving about 7in (18cm)
open at lower edge.
Sew button to left front of yoke and make
loop on right front to correspond.

Shoestring

Feline fashion

Add a few embroidery stitches to a plain black turtleneck sweater and you'll be seen in the dark.

Materials
Black, close-fitting sweater (fine machine knit)
Yellow or yellow-green stranded embroidery floss
Small tapestry needle
Dressmaker's marking pencil
Piece of cardboard about 10in (25cm) square
Small embroidery hoop and scraps of batiste or lawn (optional)

1 Mark the center front at the neckline and lower edge. Baste from one to the other to mark the center front. (Use the tapestry needle for all stitching to avoid splitting the threads of the sweater.)

2 Place the piece of cardboard under the front of the sweater to provide a firm surface and, using the dressmaker's pencil, draw the eyes and whiskers. Position the eyes about 4-6in (10-15cm) below the neck (taking care to avoid the bustline) and about 4in (10cm) apart, remembering that the sweater will stretch a little when it is worn, which will make the eyes seem further apart. Use the line of basting as a guide to centering the design.

3 To make the embroidery easier to work, baste the part of the design you are stitching to a piece of batiste or lawn; then mount the backing fabric *only* in an embroidery frame. Work the stitches through both sweater and backing fabric, then cut the fabric away, close to the stitches.

4 Using three strands of embroidery floss, embroider the eyes and whiskers in long and short stitch (see this Volume, page 82) and stem stitch (see Volume 4, page 75) respectively.

Making a bias fabric

This type of work is sometimes called "diagonal knitting" as the stitches run diagonally instead of vertically in the fabric. The main design components of a bias fabric are the increase and decrease; they are always separated in a row and this creates a diagonal line with the stitches lying toward the decrease.
Remember three rules of bias knitting and you will be able to create fabrics of your own: (1) an increase and a decrease are both necessary, (2) always separate them with several stitches and (3) the increase and decrease always appear vertically above their own kind.

1 Cast on any number of stitches. Working in stockinette stitch, decrease at the beginning of each right-side row by knitting 2 stitches together, then knit until one stitch remains. Make an invisible increase by picking up the loop lying between the stitches and knitting into the back of it; slip the last stitch.

2 All wrong-side rows are simply purled. To make a right-slanting bias you must always decrease at the beginning and increase at the end of each right-side row. The fabric need not be stockinette stitch, for all fabrics run diagonally when treated in this way. Reversible fabrics such as garter stitch and seed stitch are very popular for scarves.

3 In the finished fabric the side edges are straight while the cast-on and bound-off edges are sloping down toward the right. Single-width bias fabrics such as this are popular for scarves and shawls, rather than garments.

4 To make a left-slanting bias fabric you must increase at the beginning and decrease at the end of right-side rows as follows: slip the first stitch and make an invisible increase by picking up the loop between stitches. Work to the last 2 stitches, then slip one knit one and pass the slipped stitch over.

5 Again, all the wrong-side rows are purled. A different type of decrease is used on both left and right bias fabrics so that the chain line of bias stitches is continued.

Simple stripes introduced into a bias fabric will appear as diagonal lines of color when the fabric edges are joined. Here three-row stockinette stitch stripes also look attractive on the wrong side where there are broken lines of color.

A reversible fabric such as garter stitch is best if you want to make a scarf. The narrow stripes in this fabric look equally attractive on the right and wrong sides.

Stripes need not be formed by changing color; by using different yarn textures you can also produce a diagonal, striped fabric. For maximum effect use a highly-textured yarn, such as the bouclé shown here, against a smooth one.

Patterns in bias knitting

A number of patterned fabrics incorporate bias units. They are often repeating patterns with a number of "straight" stitches forming vertical lines and separating the slanting bias panels to give a type of rib formation.

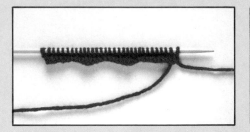

1 To make a bias repeating pattern with panels slanting to the left, cast on a multiple of 8 plus 7 extra stitches.
1st row K1, *pick up loop lying between needles and K tbl—called make 1—, K3, K2 tog, K3, rep from * ending with K1 instead of K3, **2nd row** P to end.

2 Repeat the last 2 rows for the required depth. As you work, the lower edge becomes indented. The finished effect is a type of rib pattern formed by alternating left bias panels and vertical lines of straight stitches.

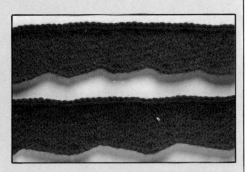

3 A similar type of fabric can be made with bias panels slanting to the right. Decrease at the beginning of a panel by slipping a stitch, knitting one, then passing the slipped stitch over; make a stitch at the end of the panel.

4 When using this type of fabric for a garment, you can achieve a more symmetrical effect if you make the bias sections in two halves of a section of knitting run in opposite directions. This also equalizes the "pull" of the bias.

5 Various effects can easily be produced by altering the number of straight stitches between bias panels. The versions here show narrow, straight panels at the top and wide ones below.

Alternative bias fabric

Another way of creating a fabric in which the stitches run diagonally is based on a square. You begin knitting with a few stitches at one corner and increase to the widest part, which is a diagonal row connecting two corners of the square. Decreases are then worked to reach the last corner.

The squares are usually sewn together to make a larger fabric or a garment: see the pattern for a jacket in Volume 2, pages 36 and 37, which is an exercise in increasing and decreasing. Large squares can be adapted to form main sections of a garment with a distinct diagonal bias.

Squares such as the one shown here usually begin with 3 cast-on stitches. You must increase at each end of every right-side row until the sides are the required length. Then decrease, again on every right-side row, to the original number of stitches.

If you turn the square slightly so that one point (corner) forms the lower edge it becomes a diamond with the stitches running in vertical lines. You can make diagonal stripes across the square simply by working normal horizontal stripes as you are knitting.

Another type of diagonal stripe that looks very attractive is simple to work and is all in one color. Alternating bands of smooth stockinette stitch and ridged reve e stockinette stitch provide an interesting contrast of textures.

Sweater with bias textured stripes

Practice bias knitting while you make this sweater in simple garter stitch. A cream knitting worsted and a matching bouclé yarn have been combined to make a sweater that is as soft and wooly as a newborn lamb.

Sizes
To fit 32[34:36:38]in (83[87:92:96]cm bust.
Length, 25½[25½:26¼:26¼]in (65[65:67:67]cm).
Sleeve seam, 16½in (42cm).
Note Directions for larger sizes are in brackets [ ]; if there is only one set of figures it applies to all sizes.

Materials
20[20:22:24]oz (550:550:600:650]g) of a medium-weight bouclé
8[8:10:10]oz (200[200:250:250]g) of a knitting worsted
1 pair each Nos. 6 and 8 (4½ and 5½mm) knitting needles
3 buttons

Gauge
13 sts and 24 rows to 4in (10cm) with knitting worsted in garter st worked on No. 8 (5½mm) needles.

Right front
**Using No. 8 (5½mm) needles and bouclé, cast on 2 sts.
Next row K to end.
Next row K twice into first st, K to last st, K twice into last st. 2 sts increased.
Rep last 2 rows until there are 30[34:38:42] sts.
Cut off bouclé and join on knitting worsted. Cont to inc on alternate rows until there are 40[44:48:52] sts. Cut off knitting worsted and join on bouclé. **
Next row K2 tog, K to last st, K twice into last st.
Next row K to end.
***Rep last 2 rows 8 times more. Cut off bouclé and join on knitting worsted. Rep previous 2 rows 5 times more. Cut off knitting worsted and join on bouclé. Cont to dec and inc at ends of alternate rows as before until longest edge measures 22¾[22¾:23½:23½]in (58[58:60:60]cm). Bind off.

Left front
Work as for right front from ** to **.
Next row K twice into first st, K to last 2 sts, K2 tog.
Next row K to end.
Complete as for right front from *** to end, reversing shaping as shown.

Waistband
Join center front seam. Using No. 6 (4½mm) needles, knitting worsted and with RS facing, pick up and K 84[88:92:96] sts along lower edge. Work 17 rows K1, P1 ribbing. Bind off in ribbing.

Left back
Work as for right front.

Right back
Work as for left front. Join center back seam and work waistband as for front.

Right yoke
Using No. 8 (5½mm) needles and knitting worsted, cast on 4 sts. Cont in garter st, inc one st at each end of every other row until there are 22[24:26:28] sts.
Next row K twice into first st, K9[10:11:12], K twice into each of next 2 sts, K9[10:11:12], K twice into last st. Cont to inc at each end of every other row until there are 42[44:46:48] sts.
Next row K twice into first st, K19[20:21:22], K twice into each of next 2 sts, K19[20:21:22], K twice into last st. Cont to inc on alternate rows until there are 50[52:54:56] sts.

Shape neck
Next row Work 24[26:28:30], turn and leave rem sts on a holder.
Complete front neck first.
Next row Bind off 6 sts, K to end. Inc one st at beg and dec one st at end of next and foll 5 alternate rows. Cont to inc at lower edge only until there are 22[24:26:28] sts.
Next row (buttonhole row) K1[2:2:2], (bind off 2, K7[7:8:9]) twice, bind off 2, K1[2:2:2].
Next row K to end, casting on 2 sts over those bound off in previous row.
K 1 row. Bind off. Rejoin yarn to neck edge of sts on holder, K to end. Keeping neck edge straight, inc one st at lower edge of yoke on next and every other row until 18 rows in all have been worked. Bind off.

Simon Butcher

RIGHT
BACK

LEFT
BACK

22¾[22¾:23½:23½]in

SLEEVE

RIGHT
YOKE

LEFT
YOKE

SLEEVE
10½[11:12¼:
13½]in

17¼[17¾:19:
20¼]in

RIGHT
FRONT

LEFT
FRONT

16½ in

8¾[9½:10¼:11]in

Left yoke

Work as for right yoke, omit buttonholes.

Collar

Join center back seam of yoke. Using No. 6 (4mm) needles, knitting worsted and with RS facing, beg at lower edge of bound-off sts on right neck, pick up and K 6 sts from bound-off sts, 34[36:40:44] sts across back neck and 6 sts from bound-off sts on left front.

Next row *K1, P1, rep from * to end, pick up and K 2 sts from neck edge, turn. Rep last row 5 times more.

Change to No. 8 (5mm) needles. Cont in ribbing, working 2 more sts from neck edge at end of every row until all sts are worked to within ½in (1cm) of center front opening. Bind off loosely in ribbing.

Sleeves

Using No. 6 (4½mm) needles and knitting worsted, cast on 34[36:40:44] sts. Work 18 rows K1, P1 ribbing. Change to No. 8 (5½mm) needles. Cont in garter st, inc one st at each end of 7th and every foll 6th row until there are 56[58:62:66] sts. Cont straight until work measures 16½in

(42cm). Bind off 8 sts at beg of next 4 rows. Bind off rem 24[26:30:34] sts.

To finish

Press or block, do not press garter st sections. Sew front and back yoke in place, lapping buttonholes over button border. Set in sleeves. Join side/sleeve seams. Sew on buttons.

Sewing / COURSE 83

*Contrast faced pleats
*Channel seam
*Pattern for a casual jacket:
  adapting the pattern;
  directions for making

Contrast faced pleats

A series of pleats faced in a contrasting fabric or color, as shown on the jacket on page 57, provides an unusual design feature. These pleats run the length of the jacket back and are stitched horizontally at strategic points to hold them in place. The stitching is optional, and if you are using this technique on a skirt, it is more suitable to omit it and simply top-stitch the pleats with vertical lines from waist to hip level only. The pleats on the jacket are reversed at the center back, making a box pleat at this point with pleats facing away from the center back on each side. We have matched the color of the facings to the pocket linings and inset strip of the channel seams, but the facings could instead be linked to other details such as the collar, cuffs or pockets. They could also be graduated in color.

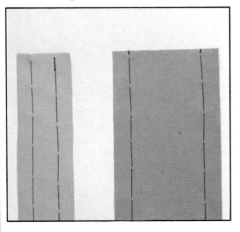

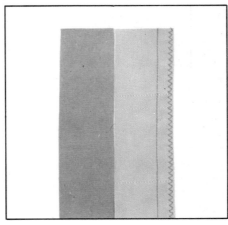

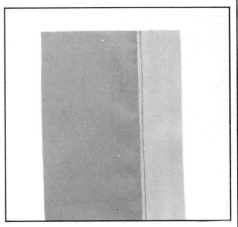

1 Mark seamlines on both long edges of each piece (panel and facing) with tailor's chalk or basting. If fabric has a right and wrong side, mark it with tailor's chalk on the wrong side.

2 With right sides together, baste and stitch facing piece to panel piece along its length. Remove basting. Press. Finish raw edges together.

3 Open seam out flat. Press seam allowances toward facing. Understitch facing to seam allowances.

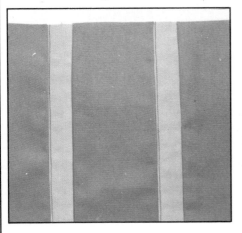

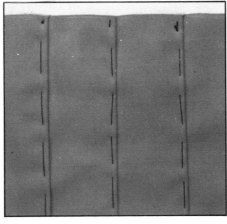

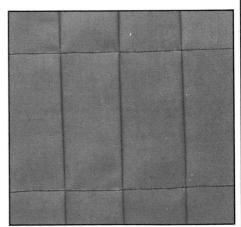

4 Join free edge of facing piece to next panel piece. Press. Finish raw edges together. Assemble and complete all panel and facing pieces in this way.

5 Fold pleats in place and baste through all thicknesses at outer edge of pleats (pleat foldlines). On the jacket on page 57, the pleats face away from each side of the center back.

6 Baste along top and bottom of folded pleats. Mark horizontal stitching lines for holding pleats. Baste and stitch along these lines using one or two rows of machine stitching. Remove all vertical basting. Press.

Simon Butcher

Channel seam

This is a strong method of joining two sections of a garment together, because the stress is taken by a separate piece of fabric (the channel) stitched to each section. The channel can be self-colored (to match the jacket), or in a contrasting color to give an interesting flash effect.

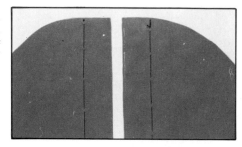

1 Cut the seam allowance of each section to twice the usual width: 1¼in (3cm) (usual width ⅝in [1.5cm]). Mark the seam allowance of each piece with a row of basting stitches.

2 Fold the seam allowance to the wrong side and baste through both thicknesses, half the width of the seam allowance from fold. For 1¼in (3cm) allowance, stitch ⅝in (1.5cm) from fold.

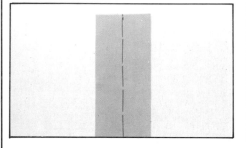

3 Cut a strip of fabric for the channel the length of the pieces to be joined by twice the width of one seam allowance: 2½in (6cm) wide for 1¼in (3cm) seam allowance. Mark the center of the strip with basting stitches all along the length.

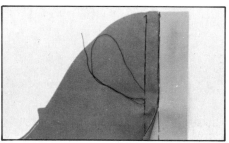

4 Lay the channel strip flat, right side up, and place one section of the piece to be seamed on top, also right side up, with the folded edge exactly matching the basted center line of the strip. Baste through all thicknesses on the marked seamline ⅝in (1.5cm) from the fold.

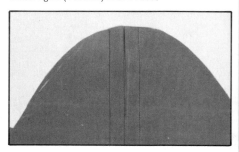

5 Repeat with the other section. Stitch through all thicknesses of each section, following the basted lines ⅝in (1.5cm) from the folded edges. Remove all basting stitches and press. Finish seam allowances together.

Casual jacket

Clever contrasting fabric details such as faced pleats, lined pockets and channel seams take this jacket into the realms of gold medal couture; the buckle and zipper and the roomy pockets are very practical too. Here we have made the jacket in satin, but you could make it in a warmer or more hardwearing fabric to suit your own fashion image.

Adapting the pattern

Measurements

The pattern for this jacket is made by altering the pattern for the basic shirt from the Stitch by Stitch Pattern Pack, available in sizes 10 to 20, which correspond to sizes 8 to 18 in ready-made clothes.

Materials
3 sheets of tracing paper 36×40in (90×100cm)
Flexible curve
Yardstick, right triangle

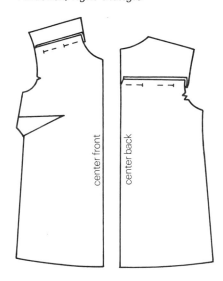

1 To make the front and back pattern, pin the shirt front and back yokes to the shirt front and back, aligning the seamlines. Trace both complete pieces.

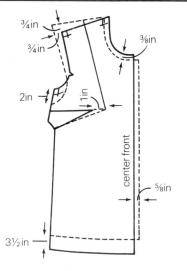

2 On the front pattern, raise and extend the shoulder cutting line by ¾in (2cm). Draw the new shoulder cutting line, tapering into the original cutting line at the neck edge. Lower the underarm curve by measuring down the side seamline from the underarm cutting line 2in (5cm).

3 Using a flexible curve, connect this point to the new shoulder cutting line. Mark the seamline. Extend the top dart line in toward the center front 1in (2.5cm) and redraw lower dart line to this point. From here draw a line up to the center of the new shoulder line.

4 Make the neckline larger by taking off $\frac{3}{8}$in (1cm) all around neck edge. Mark the new seamline. Shorten the pattern by $3\frac{1}{2}$in (9cm) at lower edge. A $\frac{5}{8}$in (1.5cm) hem allowance has been included at the lower edge. Add $\frac{5}{8}$in (1.5cm) to the center front edge.

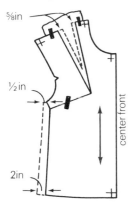

5 Cut down the line from shoulder to dart point. Close the bust dart and tape in place. This will open the pattern at the shoulder. Insert and tape paper behind the slash. Add $\frac{5}{8}$in (1.5cm) seam allowance to both cut edges of the dart. At the side seam, add $\frac{1}{2}$in (1.3cm) at underarm and 2in (5cm) at lower edge. Redraw the side cutting line. Mark $\frac{5}{8}$in (1.5cm) seam allowances. Mark the grain line parallel to the center front edge.

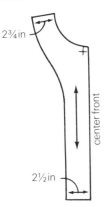

6 For the front neck facing pattern, trace front edge of new pattern piece. Trace along the lower edge for $2\frac{1}{2}$in (6.5cm) and along shoulder cutting line for $2\frac{3}{4}$in (7cm). Using a flexible curve on the upper part, draw the outer edge of the facing by connecting shoulder to lower edge as shown. Mark seamlines and grain line as shown.

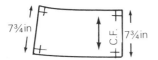

7 For the pocket pattern, lay tracing paper over the lower part of the front

Victor Yuan

pattern piece. Trace the lower edge and the front and side cutting lines to a depth of 7¾in (19.5cm). Mark this measurement at intervals across the tracing and connect for top edge of pocket. A ⅝in (1.5cm) seam allowance has been included on top and bottom edges. Mark the seam allowances and the grain line parallel to the center front.

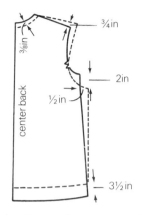

8 For the back pattern, raise and extend the shoulder cutting line at armhole edge by ¾in (2cm). Lower the armholes at the side seam, widen the neck and shorten the pattern using the same measurements and directions as for the front. At the new underarm curve, add ½in (1.3cm) to side cutting line and redraw the cutting line, tapering into the original line at the lower edge.

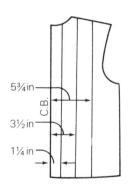

9 A series of pleat lines is marked on the back pattern piece and traced for the back panels and pleat allowances. Mark the pleat positioning lines, measuring from the center back each time and keeping the lines parallel, at 1¼, 3½ and 5¾in (3, 9, 15cm).

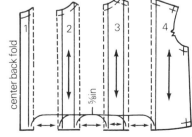

John Hutchinson

10 Trace the back panels. The first will be the center back panel and will be placed

on a fold. Add ⅝in (1.5cm) seam allowance to the long edge. The second and third are the middle back panels and will be cut twice each. Add ⅝in (1.5cm) seam allowances to both long edges. The fourth is the side back panel and will be cut twice. Add ⅝in (1.5cm) seam allowance to the inner edge.

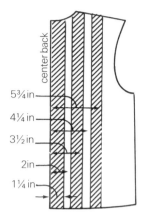

11 Another set of lines—for the pleat facings—is marked on the back pattern, parallel to the center back. Measuring from the center back each time, these are 1¼, 3½ and 5¾in (3, 9 and 15cm) (already marked), 2in (5cm) and 4¼in (11cm). Shade in the areas of the pleat facings as shown and trace these panels.

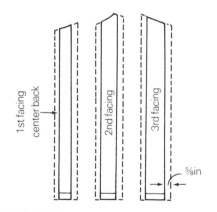

12 Add ⅝in (1.5cm) to each long edge of each panel and mark them 1, 2 and 3 for easy reference. Mark the grain lines parallel to each long edge and the seamlines at top and bottom. Each piece will be cut twice.

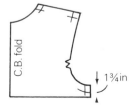

13 For the back yoke lining pattern, lay a piece of tracing paper over the top part of the complete back pattern piece and trace the center back, new neck edge, new shoulder and armhole edges and side cutting line to 1¾in (4.5cm). Draw a

line across to center back. Mark seamlines and center back as shown.

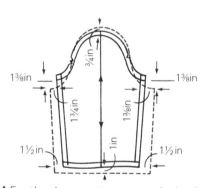

14 For the sleeve pattern, trace the basic shirt sleeve pattern, leaving extra paper around all edges. Extend grain line to top and bottom edges of pattern. Mark seamlines around all edges. Raise sleeve cap by measuring ¾in (2cm) from seamline.
15 Lower underarm seam on each side by 1⅜in (3.5cm) measuring from the armhole cutting lines. Extend the front sleeve out by 1⅜in (3.5cm) and the back by 1¾in (4.5cm) for a size 10, adding ¼in (5mm) for each larger size, measuring from the underarm cutting lines.
16 Using a flexible curve, draw the new sleeve cap seamline from the center of the sleeve cap to the marks at the underarm edges. The underarm extensions will change for larger sizes and the measurement of the sleeve cap seamline must be checked against the armhole size of front and back pieces allowing ¾in (2cm) extra for ease.
17 At the lower edge of the sleeve pattern add 1in (2.5cm) to length. To make the sleeve wider at the lower edge add 1½in (4cm) to each side. Draw the new underarm seamlines from the lower edge up to the new underarm curve.

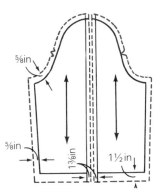

18 Add $\frac{5}{8}$in (1.5cm) seam allowance to both underarm edges and to the sleeve cap, and $1\frac{1}{2}$in (4cm) hem allowance to lower edge. Turn up the hem allowance and trace the side edges to the hem allowance. Cut along the new lines. To separate the sleeve into two pieces, cut along the center grain line from top to bottom edges of pattern and mark the grain line on both pieces parallel to the cut edge. Add $1\frac{1}{4}$in (3cm) seam allowance to the cut edges.

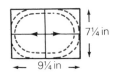

19 For the elbow patch pattern, draw a rectangle $7\frac{1}{4} \times 9\frac{1}{4}$in (18.5 × 23.5cm). Draw two lines crossing through the center of the rectangle to the outer edges. For the rounded corners, curve the outer line at one corner as shown. Then duplicate the curved line at each corner by folding the pattern on the crossing lines and cutting. Mark the $\frac{5}{8}$in (1.5cm) seam allowances and grain lines.

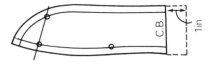

20 For the collar band pattern, trace the basic collar band, leaving extra paper at the center back edge. Draw a line through the center front as shown. The length of the collar band must be altered to fit the enlarged neckline: measure along the front and back neck seamlines on the jacket front and back pieces. Then measure along the neck edge of the collar band from center front to center back. Add the difference between the two measurements to the center back edge of the collar band. For a size 10 this will be 1in (2.5cm).

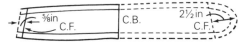

21 Fold the paper over the collar band at the center back edge and trace the

collar band shape on the paper. Open out the pattern. To the center front edge of the traced half, add $2\frac{1}{2}$in (6.5cm) for extension, rounding the edge as shown. Add $\frac{5}{8}$in (1.5cm) seam allowance to the other center front edge. Mark the other seamline and grain line.

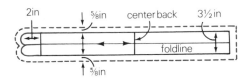

22 For the hip band pattern, draw a rectangle $3\frac{1}{2}$in (9cm) wide by the total hip measurement plus $1\frac{3}{4}$in (4.5cm) ease allowance, for the length. Mark the center back in the center of the rectangle and the foldline along the center of the rectangle. At one end add 2in (5cm) and mark the foldline. Round the end of one half of the band as shown.
23 Fold the band in half along the foldline and trace the rounded end on the other half of the band. Add $\frac{5}{8}$in (1.5cm) seam allowance to all edges. Mark the seamlines.

Directions for making

Suggested fabrics
Linen, heavy cotton, satin, corduroy, denim, vinyl.

Materials
45in (115cm)-wide fabric with or
without nap:
Size 10: $2\frac{5}{8}$yd (2.4m)
Size 12: $2\frac{3}{4}$yd (2.5m)
Sizes 14, 16: $2\frac{7}{8}$yd (2.6m)
Sizes 18, 20: $3\frac{1}{8}$yd (2.8m)
45in (115cm)-wide fabric for
contrasting sections:
For all sizes: $\frac{3}{4}$yd (.7m)
36in (90cm)-wide lining:
For all sizes: $\frac{3}{4}$yd (.7m)
36in (90cm)-wide interfacing:
For all sizes: $\frac{3}{4}$yd (.7m)
Matching thread
20in (51cm) open-ended zipper
One $1\frac{3}{4}$in (4.5cm) half-buckle (one
straight side)
One $1\frac{1}{2}$in (4cm) half-buckle
Metal eyelet kit
Shoulder pads (optional)

1 With right sides together, pin, baste and stitch the shoulder darts. Finish and press darts open.

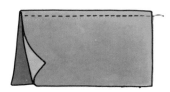

2 With right sides together, pin, baste and stitch the pocket and pocket lining together along the top edge only. Trim the seam allowance.

3 Turn pocket right side out and baste along stitched edge. Press. Topstitch along this edge, stitching $\frac{1}{4}$in (5mm) in from stitched edge. Press.

4 With right sides on top, baste the pockets to the jacket fronts, matching the lower edges, center front edges and side edges.
5 Run two rows of gathering stitches along the lower edge of the fronts, stitching through pocket, pocket lining and front section, to within 2in (5cm) of the center front and side seams.

6 Turn under the $\frac{5}{8}$in (1.5cm) seam allowance along the center front edges of the jacket and baste. Press flat.
7 Pin and baste the zipper in the center front opening.

Terry Evans

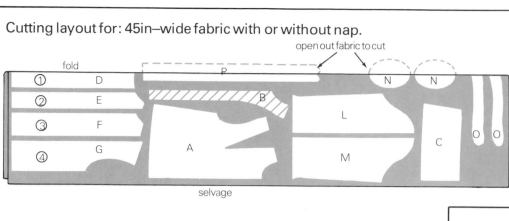

Cutting layout for: 45in—wide fabric with or without nap.

fold

open out fabric to cut

① D
② E
③ F
④ G

P

B

L

M

A

C

N   N

O O

selvage

45in-wide fabric with or without nap. (contrast)

fold

channel strip

① H
② I
③ J

selvage

36in-wide lining.

fold

K

C

selvage

36in-wide interfacing

fold

cut 1

O

P

hip band cut in two pieces

selvage

Ian Stephen

Key to adapted pieces

A	Jacket front	Cut 2
B	Front neck facing	Cut 2
C	Pocket	Cut 2
D	Center back panel (1)	Cut 1 on fold
E	Back panel (2)	Cut 2
F	Back panel (3)	Cut 2
G	Side back panel (4)	Cut 2
H	Center back pleat facing (1)	Cut 2 contrast
I	Back pleat facing (2)	Cut 2 contrast
J	Back pleat facing (3)	Cut 2 contrast
K	Back yoke lining	Cut 1 on fold
L	Sleeve front	Cut 2
M	Sleeve back	Cut 2
N	Elbow patch	Cut 2
O	Collar band	Cut 2
P	Hip band	Cut 1

Lining: Use pieces **C** and **K**
Interfacing: Use pieces **O** and **P** (half) — allow extra length for joining two pieces of hip band.
Contrast channel strip: Cut 2 to sleeve center seam length × $1\frac{1}{4}$in (3cm) wide.

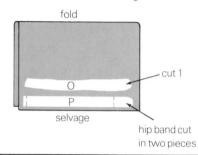

8 Finish the outer edge of the front facing by turning under $\frac{1}{4}$in (5mm) and machine stitching. Press. Turn under the seam allowance along the center front edges of facings and baste. Press flat.

10 From the right side, stitch the zipper and facings in place, stitching $\frac{3}{8}$in (1cm) from center front edges. Press.
11 Join back panels and facings and form pleats as described on page 55.

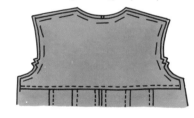

14 With wrong sides together and neck, shoulder and armhole edges matching, baste the back yoke lining to the inside of jacket back.
15 With right sides together baste and stitch the shoulder and side seams, keeping the front facings free at the shoulder. Finish seams and then press them open.

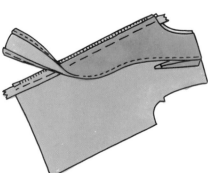

9 With wrong sides together and front and neck edges matching, baste the front edges and front facings to the inside of the jacket fronts over the zipper tape and around the neck edge.

12 With right side on top, run three rows of topstitching across the back pleats, positioning the first row $5\frac{1}{2}$in (14cm) below the center back neck seamline and the other two at equally spaced intervals. Press.
13 Finish the lower edge of the back yoke lining by turning in $\frac{1}{4}$in (5mm) and machine stitching. Press.

16 At the shoulders turn under the shoulder seam allowance of the facings

and slip stitch to the shoulder seam allowance of jacket. Press.

17 Baste the interfacing to the wrong side of one collar band section. With right sides together, baste and stitch the two collar band pieces together along the top edge and curved end to the center front only. Clip the neck seam allowance at the center front at the end of the stitching as shown. Trim the interfacing close to stitching. Trim seam allowance.

18 Turn the collar right side out and baste along stitched edge. Press.

19 With right sides together and center front points and center back points matching, pin and baste the interfaced edge of the collar to the jacket neck edge. Stitch the seam.
20 Trim the interfacing close to stitching. Grade the seam allowance and clip the curved edges. Press the seam toward the collar.

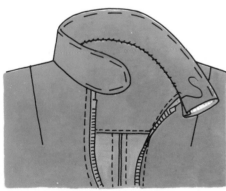

21 On the inside turn under the seam allowance of the free edge of collar and slip stitch it to the stitching line. Press.

22 At the center front edge of the left side of collar, turn in the seam allowance of the top collar and press. Attach an

eyelet to the under-collar seam allowance, in the center of the seamline.

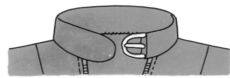

23 Slip the buckle prong through the eyelet and bring the seam allowance over the buckle and slip inside collar.

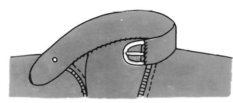

24 Slip stitch the two collar edges together holding the buckle firmly in place. On the right collar extension attach one eyelet at the center front as shown.

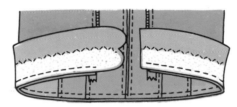

25 Join the two hip band interfacings together to form one long piece. Baste interfacing to wrong side of one half of hip band and catch-stitch it to foldline.
26 With right sides together and center fronts and center backs matching, pin the interfaced edge of the band to the lower edge, pulling up the gathering threads until the jacket fronts fit the band. Baste, spreading gathers evenly. Stitch seam. Trim interfacing and grade seam allowances. Press seam allowance toward the band.

27 Fold band, right sides together, along the foldline and stitch around the curved end to the center front as shown. Trim interfacing and seam allowance.

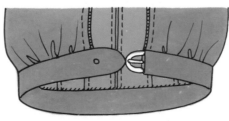

28 Turn the band right side out and baste along folded edge. Press. On the inside

turn under the seam allowance of the free edge of band and slip stitch to the stitching line.
29 At the straight end of the band, attach the buckle as directed for the collar. Attach the eyelet to the right extension as before.

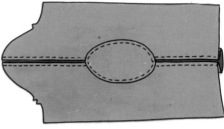

30 Turn under the seam allowance around the edges of the two elbow patches and baste. Press flat.
31 Make the channel seam in the sleeve (see page 56). Try on sleeve and mark the elbow position in the center of the sleeve. With wrong side of patch to right side of sleeve, pin and baste the elbow patch in the position marked, centered over the channel seam. Stitch $\frac{1}{4}$in (5mm) in from edge. Press.

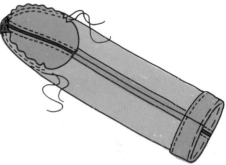

32 With right sides together, baste and stitch the underarm seam of sleeve. Finish and press seam open. Prepare the sleeve cap for easing in fullness. Finish the lower edge of sleeve by turning in $\frac{1}{4}$in (5mm) and machine stitching. Press.
33 Turn the hem allowance up to the inside of sleeve and baste around lower edge. Press. Sew hem to sleeve.

34 With right sides together and shoulder point and seams matching, pin the sleeve into armhole, easing fullness to fit. Baste and machine stitch sleeve in place with sleeve on top. Trim seam allowance, clip curved edges and press seam toward the sleeve. Finish seams together. Make or buy a pair of shoulder pads and sew to the inside edge of shoulders (see Volume 9, page 60).

Sewing / COURSE 84

*Leather-bound slit pockets
*Suspender ends
*Elasticized shoulder straps
*Pattern for a skirt with a bib:
 adapting the pattern;
 directions for making

Leather-bound slit pockets

An attractive feature on many types of garment is a slit pocket bound in leather; it is sensible too, as the pocket is extra strong and hard-wearing and therefore ideally suited to overalls. The pockets shown here are reinforced at each end with a triangular piece of leather and are design-linked to the bib and shoulder straps of the skirt on page 65. (Real or imitation leather can be used.)

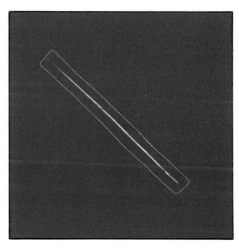

1 Stay stitch around the pocket position, stitching ¼in (5mm) to each side of the positioning line. Cut along the center of the opening.

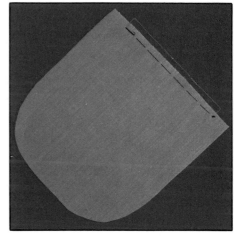

2 Trim the seam allowance along the straight edge of the top pocket bag to ¼in (5mm). With wrong sides together, baste the top pocket bag to the inside of the garment on the lower seamline of the pocket, matching the straight edges and overlapping opening at each end.

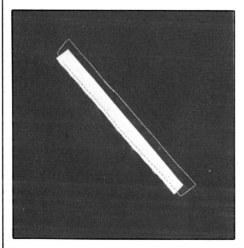

3 Cut two strips of leather, each ¾in (2cm) wide by the length of the pocket opening. With right side on top fold leather strip in half lengthwise over the raw edge of the opening and the pocket bag, enclosing the raw edges inside. From the right side, baste and stitch the strip in place through all thicknesses close to the cut edges of the leather. Remove basting.

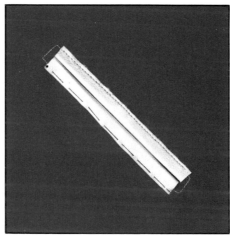

4 Fold the other strip in half lengthwise over the other raw edge of the opening and baste it in place through all thicknesses.

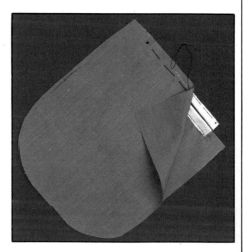

5 With the right sides of the pocket bags together, matching the seamline of the upper pocket bag to the pocket opening line, baste the pocket bag in place along the top edge.

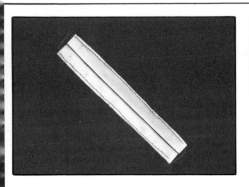

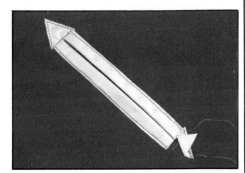

6 From the right side, stitch leather strip and back pocket bag in place, stitching close to the cut edges of the leather. Remove basting.

7 On the inside, baste and stitch the two pocket bag pieces together. Press. Finish the raw edges of the bags together.

8 Trace and cut out two leather triangles from the outline pattern given on page 67. On the right side, place the long edge of one leather triangle across one end of the pocket opening. Baste and stitch in place, stitching close to all edges of the triangle. Repeat with other end. This will reinforce the pocket.

Suspender ends

Genuine suspender ends are used to fasten the straps to the bib of the skirt on page 65. Here they are made in gold-effect imitation leather with a reinforcing triangle above each strap, but you could make them in matching leather, suede or any material which does not ravel and is fairly strong.

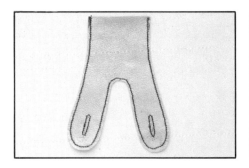

1 Trace and cut out four shapes following the outline for the suspender ends given on page 67. Trace and cut out two triangles for the straps from pattern on the same page.
For each suspender end, place two cut pieces together with wrong sides facing. Glue and stitch together, as close as possible to all edges. Mark and stitch around each buttonhole close to the edges. Cut buttonholes open.

2 Make the shoulder straps, leaving one end open. Turn in the seam allowance at the opening end and press flat.

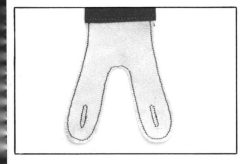

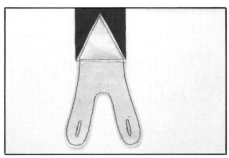

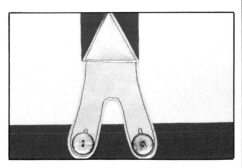

3 Slip ⅝in (1.5cm) of the straight edge of the suspender end into the open end of the strap and stitch across this end, securing the end inside the strap.

4 With right sides on top, and the end of the triangle across the end of the strap, baste and stitch the leather triangle in place, stitching close to the edges. Repeat with the other strap.

5 When the skirt, bib and straps are made, try garment on and attach the buttons to the right side of the bib to correspond with the buttonholes on the suspender ends (two buttons for each suspender).

Simon Butcher

63

Elasticized shoulder straps

The back ends of the straps of the skirt on page 65 are elasticized and slanted slightly for a good fit. This method can be used on any garment on which straps are incorporated as part of the design. If you cannot find elastic of the correct width, you can use two narrower pieces cut to the same length.

1 Cut two pieces of elastic the width of the finished shoulder straps (1½in [4cm] for the skirt on page 65) by 1½in (4cm) long.

2 Make the shoulder straps as directed on page 63, leaving the back ends unfinished. Slide the elastic through one end to a depth of 4in (10cm). Pin and baste in place across the width at this point. Repeat with the second strap.

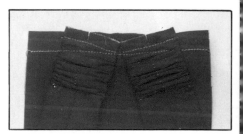

3 Stitch across the width with two close rows of stitching to hold the elastic firmly in place. Remove basting. Repeat with other strap. The elastic will be shorter than the straps at this stage.

4 Pull the end of the elastic down (or push the fabric up) to meet the raw ends of the strap. Baste and stitch ⅜in (1cm) from the raw ends to hold. This will gather the strap. Complete the second strap in the same way.
Remove basting.

5 Position straps with right sides facing on the right side of the back, slanting the strap upward slightly at the outside edges. Baste and stitch on the seamline (⅝in [1.5cm] allowed), across the top of the garment. Complete the back section following the directions on page 68.

Skirt with bib

This practical but feminine skirt with leather suspender ends and pocket trim is both hard-wearing and good-looking. Make it in denim for everyday wear, or velveteen for special occasions.

Adapting the pattern

Measurements
The pattern for the skirt is adapted from the basic skirt pattern from the Stitch by Stitch Pattern Pack, available in sizes 10 to 20, which correspond to sizes 8 to 18 in ready-made clothes.

Materials
3 sheets of tracing paper 36×40in (90×100cm)
Right triangle
Flexible curve
Yardstick

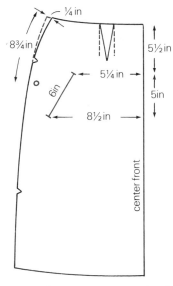

1 For the skirt front pattern, trace basic skirt. The dart allowance becomes the tuck allowance. For the width of the tuck, mark the dart lines at the waist seam.
2 Add ¼in (5mm) to the side seam edge at the waistline. Taper the side cutting line into the original cutting line at notch. Mark the bottom of zipper position at side seam 8¾in (22cm) below waist cutting line.

3 For the pocket position, measure down the center front edge from the waist cutting line 5½in (14cm) and a further 5in (12.5cm), marking each point. Draw a line across the pattern from each point. The top and bottom lines are 5¼in (13.5 cm) and 8½in (21.5cm) long respectively.
4 Connect these lines for the pocket position line as shown. It should measure approximately 6in (15cm) long.

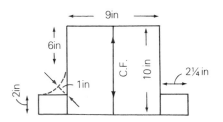

5 For the bib pattern, draw a rectangle 9in (23cm) wide by 10in (25cm) long for a size 10, adding an extra ¼in (5mm) to the length for each larger size.
6 At lower side edge of rectangle, measure out horizontally 2¼in (6cm) for a size 10, adding an extra ½in (1.3cm) for each larger size—for example 3¼in (8.5cm) for a size 14. Measure up and draw a line 2in (5cm) long at a right angle to this line; connect line to side.

7 To draw the curved edge, measure 6in (15cm) down the side edge from the top and mark. Using a flexible curve, draw the curved edge from this point to the outer corner as shown. The deepest part of the curve should be approximately 1in (2.5cm) from the inner corner.

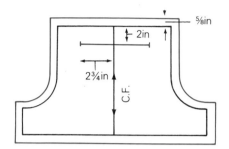

8 Fold the pattern in half along the center front line and trace the shape on the other side. The center front is on the straight grain. Mark the top positioning line for the patch pocket by measuring down the center front from the top edge 2in (5cm) and then out to each side of the center front 2¾in (7cm). Connect these points for the pocket line. Add ⅝in (1.5cm) seam allowance to all edges.

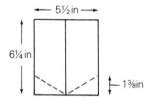

9 For the bib pocket pattern, draw a rectangle 5½ × 6¼in (14×16cm). Draw the grain line down the center of the rectangle. At the lower edge, measure up both side edges 1⅜in (3.5cm) and draw a line from each side into the center at the bottom edge, forming a point.

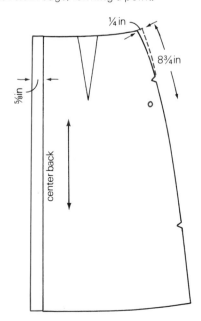

10 For the skirt back pattern, trace the

basic skirt back, adding ⅝in (1.5cm) seam allowance to the center back edge. Widen the side seam at the waistline edge and mark the zipper position, using the same measurements and directions as given for the skirt front.

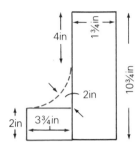

11 For the back pattern, draw a rectangle 1¾ × 10¾in (4.5 × 27.5cm) for a size 10, adding an extra ¼in (5mm) to the length for each larger size. At the lower edge, extend the line from the side by 3¾in (9.5cm) for a size 10, adding an extra ½in (1.3cm) for each larger size – for example 4¾in (12cm) for a size 14.

12 Measure up and draw a line at a right angle to this line, making it 2in (5cm) long. Connect this point back to the side edge of the back section. From the top measure down the side edge 4in (10cm) and mark. Using a flexible curve, draw the curve as shown, from this point to the outer corner. At the deepest part of the curve, the distance from the inner corner to the curved line should be approximately 2in (5cm) as shown.

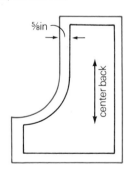

13 Add ⅝in (1.5cm) seam allowance to all edges and mark grain line parallel to the center back edge.

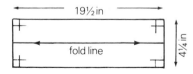

14 For the shoulder strap pattern, draw a rectangle 4¼ × 19½in (11 × 50cm) for all sizes. These measurements include ⅝in (1.5cm) seam allowances on all edges, and the length will be adjusted for smaller sizes during assembly of the garment. Mark the foldline and grain line along the center of the rectangle. Mark the seamlines.

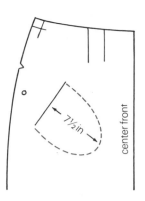

15 For the skirt pocket bag pattern, draw the shape of the pocket bag on skirt front pattern as shown; the depth of the pocket is 7½in (19cm).

16 Trace the pocket shape and mark the grain line parallel to the center front edge. Add ⅝in (1.5cm) seam allowance to curved edge and ¾in (2cm) seam allowance to the straight edge.

Directions for making

Suggested fabrics
Denim, corduroy, ticking, poplin, sailcloth, velveteen.

Materials
45in (115cm)-wide fabric without nap:
  Sizes 10, 12: 2¼yd (2m)
  Sizes 14, 16: 2⅜yd (2.1m)
  Sizes 18, 20: 2½yd (2.2m)
36in (90cm)-wide fabric without nap:
  Sizes 10, 12: 2¾yd (2.5m)
  Sizes 14, 16: 2⅞yd (2.6m)
  Sizes 18, 20: 3yd (2.7m)
36in (90cm)-wide real or fake leather:
  For all sizes: ¼yd (.2m)
Matching thread
Fabric glue
8in (20cm) skirt or dress zipper
Four ½in (.3cm)-diameter buttons
¼yd (.2m) of 1½in (4cm)-wide elastic

Note *If using fabrics with nap, allow extra yardage.*

A	Bib	Cut 1 on fold
B	Skirt front	Cut 1 on fold
C	Back	Cut 2
D	Skirt back	Cut 2
E	Bib pocket	Cut 1
F	Shoulder strap	Cut 2
G	Pocket bag	Cut 4

Leather pieces: Cut 4 suspender ends; cut 2 suspender end triangles; cut 1 back

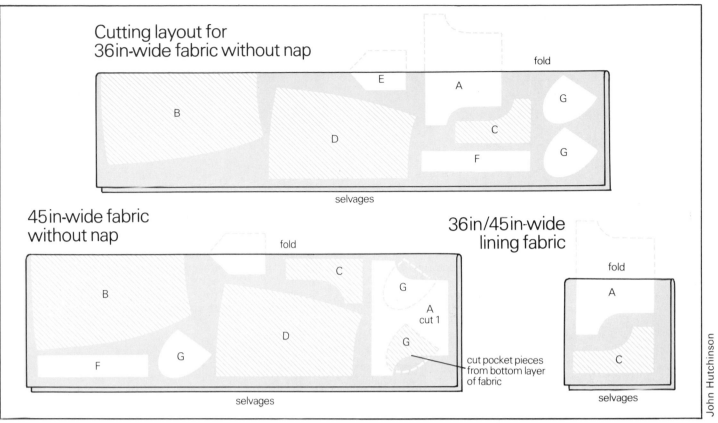

Cutting layout for 36in-wide fabric without nap

fold

E A

B

D C

F G G

selvages

45in-wide fabric without nap

fold

B C

G

D A cut 1

F G

selvages

cut pocket pieces from bottom layer of fabric

36in/45in-wide lining fabric

fold

A

C

selvages

John Hutchinson

triangle; cut 2 bib pocket triangles; cut 4 slit pocket triangles; cut 4 binding strips $6 \times \frac{3}{4}$in (15×2cm).
Lining: Use **A** Cut 1 on fold; **C** Cut 2.

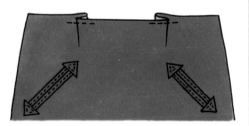

1 Fold, and baste the front waist tucks in place. Press toward side seams on right side. Make the bound slit pocket as shown on page 62.

2 Stitch and press back waist darts. With right sides together, fold, baste and stitch the center back seam of skirt. Finish and press seam open.

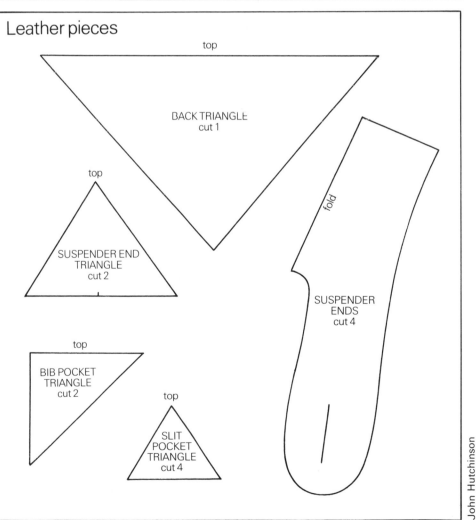

Leather pieces

top

BACK TRIANGLE cut 1

top

SUSPENDER END TRIANGLE cut 2

fold

SUSPENDER ENDS cut 4

top

BIB POCKET TRIANGLE cut 2

top

SLIT POCKET TRIANGLE cut 4

John Hutchinson

3 With right sides together, baste and stitch the skirt side seams, leaving the left side seam open for zipper. Finish and press seams open.

4 Measure around all outer edges of bib pocket and cut a strip of leather to this measurement by ¾in (2cm) wide. With wrong sides inside, fold the strip in half lengthwise over the edges of the pocket and pin in place. At each corner cut a small triangle out of the leather strip on back and front to miter the corners and keep the leather flat.

5 Baste and stitch the strip in place, stitching close to the cut edges of the leather. If necessary, to avoid pin marks, glue the leather binding in place before stitching, using a suitable glue.

6 Baste the pocket to the right side of the bib in the position indicated on the pattern. Topstitch in place as close as possible to the inner edge of the leather around the sides and lower edges of the pocket.

7 Trace and cut out two leather triangles following the trace pattern on page 67 and stitch them to the pocket through all thicknesses. The triangles should cover the top corners of pocket.

8 Baste the center seam of the back piece, and baste it to the bib at the right side. Try the bib section on and make any necessary alterations at the center back seam, keeping the top edge the same measurement, (4¾in [12cm] including seam allowances at each side).

9 Remove bib section and mark any new fitting lines. With right sides together, baste and stitch the center back seam of the back piece. Baste and stitch the bib and back together at the right side. Make bib section lining in same way.

10 With right sides together and center fronts, center backs and side seams

matching, baste and stitch the bib section to the skirt at the waistline edge. Trim seam allowance and press upward. Insert zipper into left side seam opening.

11 With right sides together, fold the straps in half lengthwise. Baste and stitch along length. Remove basting. Press seam open. Turn right side out, centering the seam. Press flat.

12 Complete straps with elastic and attach to the right side of the back piece as shown on page 64. (Adjust the length of the straps **before** making and attaching suspender ends as shown on page 63.)

13 With right sides together and edges and seams matching, baste and stitch the bib section lining to the main bib section around the edges, securing the elasticized straps at the center back as you work. Trim all seams. Clip corners and curved seam allowances. Curved seams can be strengthened with seam binding at this stage to prevent stretching during wear.

14 Turn the lining to the inside and baste around the stitched edges. Press. At the waist seam and left side seam, turn under the seam allowance of the lining and slip stitch the lining to the waist stitching line and zipper tape. Press.

15 Topstitch all edges of the bib section, stitching ⅜in (1cm) in from the edges. Topstitch around waistline, stitching ⅜in (1cm) above waist seamline. Press.

16 Trace and cut out the back triangle from the trace pattern on page 67. Baste and stitch the triangle in place at the top edge of the back piece, stitching close to the edges of the triangle as shown.

17 Complete the bib with buttons to correspond with the suspender ends and turn up the hem, completing it with a suitable stitch.

Sewing / COURSE 85

*Applying a one-piece facing to a square neckline
*Couching a motif
*Pattern for a sundress with a wrapover skirt: adapting the pattern; directions for making

Applying a one-piece facing to a square neckline

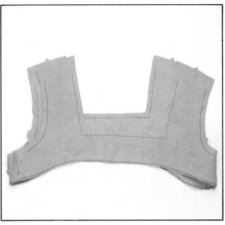

1 Staystitch the neck and armhole edges of the garment and the facing pieces to prevent these edges from stretching.

2 With right sides together, pin, baste and stitch the side seams of the garment and the facings. Finish the seam allowance on the dress and press seams open. Finish outer edges of facings. Press.

3 With right sides together and center fronts, center backs and side seams matching, baste and stitch the front and back neck and armhole facings to the garment around these edges, stitching to the shoulder seamlines only. The shoulder seams are left open. Trim the seam allowances, clip curved edges and clip into the inner corners at the neckline.

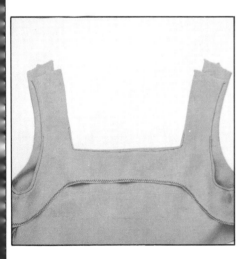

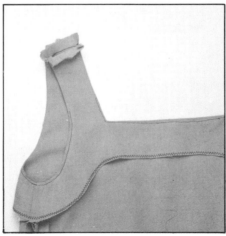

4 Turn the facings to the inside of the garment, press the seam allowances toward the facings and understitch, stitching as far as possible up the straps. Press.

5 With right sides together, baste and stitch the garment front and back and one facing seam allowance together at the shoulder seams.

6 Grade the seam allowances and press them toward the free facing seam allowance, slipping the raw edges between the facing and the main garment. Turn under the seam allowance of the free edge of the facing and slip stitch it to the stitching line, enclosing all raw edges. Press. Catch-stitch the facings to the side seam allowances.

Couching a motif

Couching is a method of outlining a motif with a laid thread. It can be used in conjunction with a filling stitch (such as the long and short stitch in Volume 18, page 76) or by itself for a simpler effect, as on the dress shown opposite. There are several different methods of couching; here we show three of the most usual.

Most threads can be couched, from fine pearl cotton or mercerized crochet cotton to heavy bouclé yarn, although not all threads are suitable for all methods.

Couching by hand

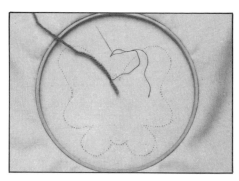

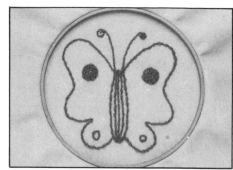

1 Start by marking the motif on the right side of the fabric, using tailor's chalk, dressmaker's carbon paper or basting stitches. Beginners should practice with a simple shape.

2 Working from the right side, with the fabric in an embroidery hoop, lay one or two thicknesses of yarn or thread over the motif at the starting point. Anchor the thread with a couple of backstitches, using a finer thread.

3 With the yarn following the outline of the motif, take tiny stitches over the yarn $\frac{1}{4}$-$\frac{1}{2}$in (5mm-1.2cm) apart. Work back to starting point, bringing in new yarn as necessary. Secure the ends on the wrong side of the fabric.

Couching by machine

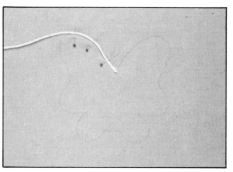

1 Mark the motif on the right side of the fabric as before.

2 Outline the motif with yarn and anchor it with pins, placing the pins at a right angle to the yarn.

3 Zig-zag over the yarn, using a narrow stitch and removing the pins as you come to them. Secure the ends.

Couching by machine (false couching)

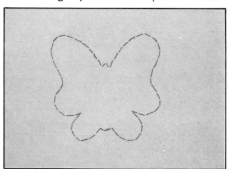

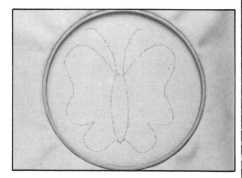

1 Mark the motif on the wrong side of the fabric, using tailor's chalk, dressmaker's carbon paper or basting stitches. A fairly fine thread must be used for this method.

2 Wind the thread which is to be couched onto the bobbin. Wind by hand, keeping the tension even. If using metallic thread, use a pencil to keep the thread flat.

3 Working from wrong side and using a long straight stitch, stitch the motif. The tension on the bobbin should be tighter than on the top. (The finished motif is shown here.)

Sundress with wrapover skirt

This pretty sundress with its embroidered motifs on bodice and skirt will see you through the summer in style—it's ideal for almost any occasion.

Adapting the pattern

Measurements
The dress is adapted from the basic dress pattern taken from the Stitch by Stitch Pattern Pack, available in sizes 10 to 20, which correspond to sizes 8 to 18 in ready-made clothes.

Materials
4 sheets of tracing paper 36 × 40in (90cm × 100cm)
Flexible curve
Right triangle
Yardstick; tracing wheel

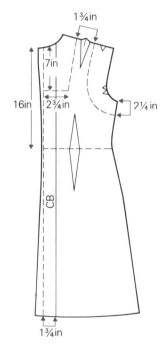

1 For the back pattern, trace the basic dress back pattern, extending the grain line to the top and bottom edges of the pattern.
2 To mark a new straight center back edge, measure out from the grain line 1¾in (4.5cm) and draw a parallel line from top to bottom edges of pattern. To find center of shoulder, measure along shoulder seamline from neck cutting line 3in (7.5cm) for sizes 10, 12; 3⅛in (8cm) for sizes 14, 16; 3¼in (8.5cm) for sizes 18, 20. Measure off ⅞in (2.3cm) to each

side of this point for the new shoulder seam (total width $1\frac{3}{4}$in [4.6cm]).

3 For the depth of the new neckline, measure down the new center back from the neck cutting line 7in (17.5cm) for a size 10, adding an extra $\frac{1}{4}$in (5mm) to this measurement for each larger size. Draw a line from this point across the pattern $2\frac{3}{4}$in (7cm) long and continue up to the new shoulder point as shown.

4 Lower the armhole at the side seam by $2\frac{1}{4}$in (6cm), measuring from the armhole cutting line. Using a flexible curve, draw the new armhole from the shoulder to the side seam as shown.

5 Mark the waistline, measuring down the center back from the original neck cutting line 16in (41cm) for a size 10, adding an extra $\frac{1}{4}$in (5mm) to this measurement for each larger size.

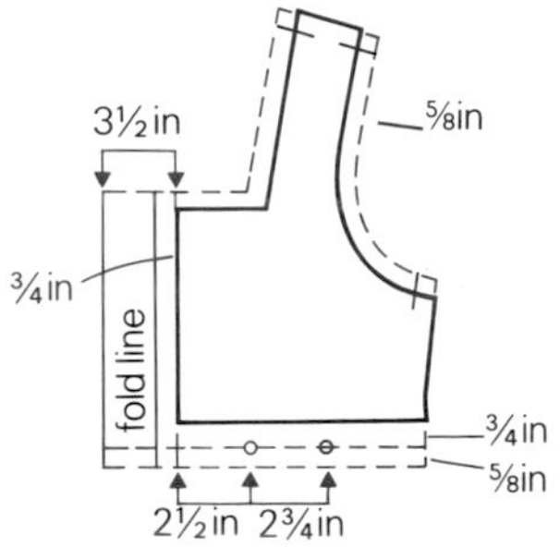

6 Trace the outline of the new bodice, leaving extra paper at the center back and lower edge. Add $3\frac{1}{2}$in (9cm) to the center back edge for the buttonhole allowance. Mark the foldline $\frac{3}{4}$in (2cm) out from the center back edge.

7 To allow for slight fullness at the waist, lengthen the lower edge of the bodice by $\frac{3}{4}$in (2cm). On this line mark the gathering positions $2\frac{1}{2}$in (6.5cm) from the center back and a further $2\frac{3}{4}$in (7cm) out. Mark the grain line parallel to the center back. Add $\frac{5}{8}$in (1.5cm) seam allowance to the new neck and armhole edges and the lower edge. The fullness at the waist will be reduced by gathering when assembling the dress.

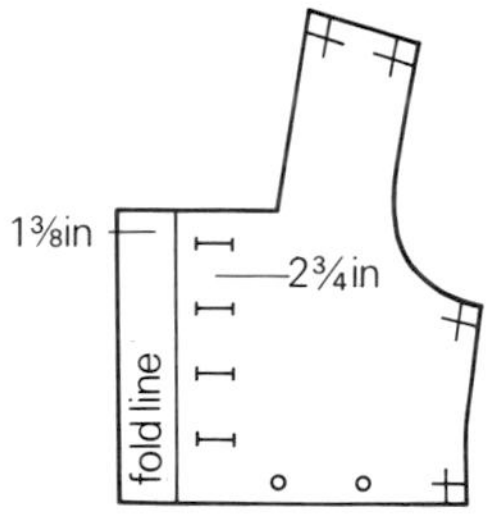

8 The horizontal buttonhole positions at the center back are $1\frac{1}{4}$in (3cm) long, and placed $\frac{5}{8}$in (1.5cm) from the foldline. The first is $1\frac{3}{8}$in (3.5cm) from the new back neck cutting line and the other three at $2\frac{3}{4}$in (7cm) intervals below the first. The skirt is fastened with a zipper.

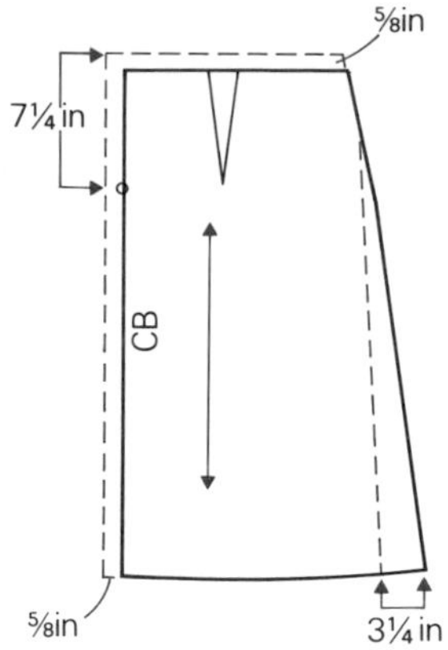

9 Trace the skirt from the new pattern. Add $\frac{5}{8}$in (1.5cm) seam allowances to the center back and waistline edges. Mark the grain line parallel to the center back edge. Mark the bottom of the zipper position at center back seam $7\frac{1}{4}$in (19.5cm) below waist cutting line.

10 To make the skirt narrower, measure in along the lower edge from the side cutting line $3\frac{1}{4}$in (8cm) and draw new side cutting line, tapering into the original line at hip level. Mark the back dart lines.

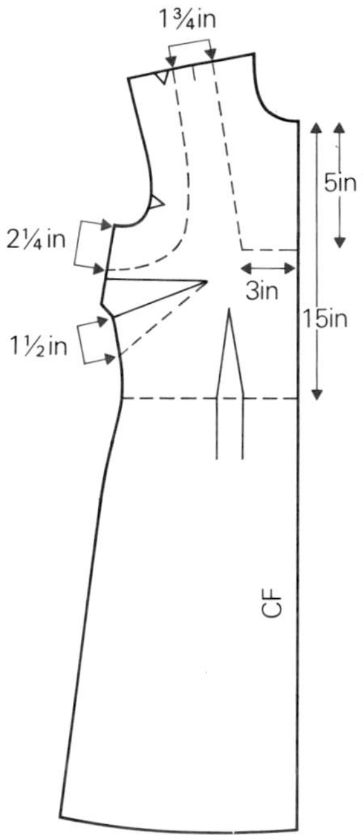

11 For the front pattern trace the basic dress front pattern. Mark the center of the shoulder seam and the width of the new shoulder line as for the back of the bodice.

12 For the depth of the new front neckline, measure down the center front edge from neck cutting line 5in (12.5cm) for a size 10, adding an extra $\frac{1}{4}$in (5mm) to this measurement for each larger size. Draw a line across the pattern from this point 3in (7.5cm) long. Draw the new inner neckline from the shoulder to this line as shown. The new neckline will be square.

13 Lower and redraw the armhole as directed for the back. Mark the waistline, measuring down the center front edge from the original neck cutting line 15in (38cm) for size 10, adding an extra $\frac{1}{4}$in (5mm) to this measurement for each larger size.

14 The angle of the side bust dart is altered. Measure down the side seam from lower dart line $1\frac{1}{2}$in (4cm) and draw a line from this point to the dart point.

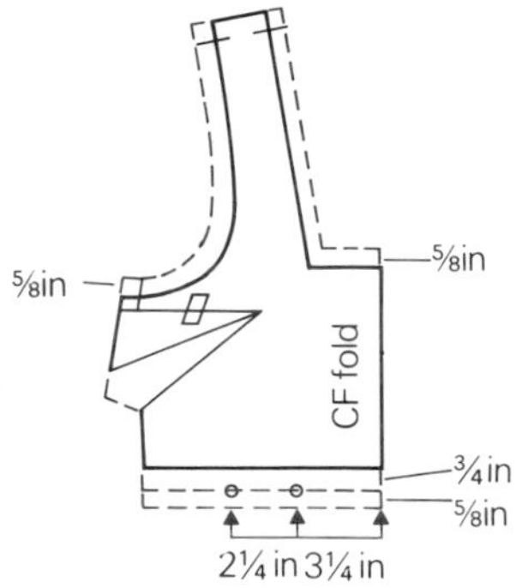

15 Trace the outline of the new bodice from the pattern, leaving extra paper at the lower edge. Cut along the new lower dart line and close the original dart, taping it in place. This will open the pattern at the new dart position.

16 Insert and tape a piece of paper behind the slash. To shape the side edge of the new dart, fold dart in place and, using a tracing wheel, mark the side cutting line. Open out the dart and draw the cutting line and seamline.

17 For slight fullness at the waist, add $\frac{3}{4}$in (2cm) to lower edge of the pattern. Add $\frac{5}{8}$in (1.5cm) seam allowance to neck and armhole edges and to lower edge. Mark the gathering positions along the seamline at the lower edge, measuring $3\frac{1}{4}$in (8cm) from the center front and then a further $2\frac{1}{4}$in (6cm).

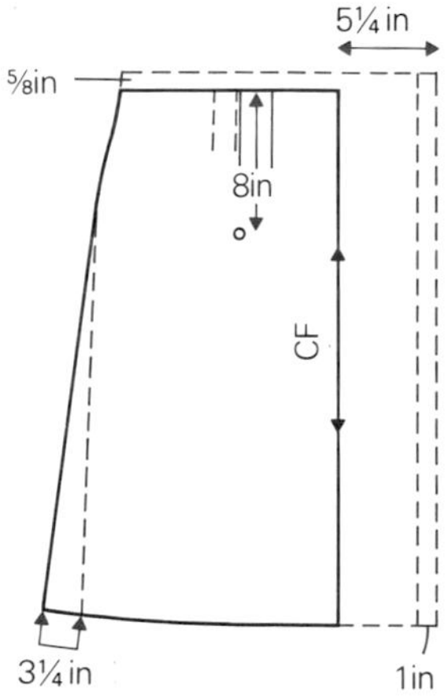

18 Trace the skirt from the new dress pattern, leaving extra paper at the center front edge. The dart allowance becomes the tuck allowance and this position is moved over toward the side. Using the outer dart line as the inner line of the tuck, mark the outer line of the tuck the same distance out as the width of the dart, as shown. To mark position of overlay flap, continue inner tuck line down for 8in (20cm) from waist seamline and mark with a circle.

19 For the wrapover, add the following measurements to center front edge: 5$\frac{1}{4}$in (13cm) for a size 10, plus an extra $\frac{1}{4}$in (5mm) for each larger size. Mark the foldline 1in (2.5cm) from this edge.

20 Make the skirt narrower by 3$\frac{1}{4}$in (8cm) at the lower side edge as for the back. Add $\frac{5}{8}$in (1.5cm) seam allowance to waistline edge. Mark the grain line at the center front.

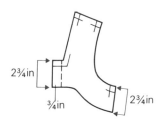

21 For the back neck and armhole facing fold the center back facing on the back bodice pattern into place. Trace the neck, shoulder, armhole and the side cutting line to 2$\frac{3}{4}$in (7cm). At the center back edge the facing will be joined to the bodice facing. Mark position of center back facing with a broken line. To this add $\frac{3}{4}$in (2cm). The width of the facing will be 2$\frac{3}{4}$in (7cm). Draw outline and mark grain line parallel to back edge.

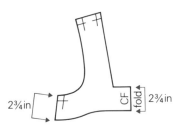

22 For front neck and armhole facing, trace the neck, shoulder and armhole edges and along center front and down side cutting line for 2$\frac{3}{4}$in (7cm). Draw the outline of the facing as shown, making the width 2$\frac{3}{4}$in (7cm). Mark the seam allowance and center front.

Directions for making

Suggested fabrics
Medium-weight linen or cotton.

Materials
36in (90cm)-wide fabric, without nap:
    Sizes 10, 12: 3$\frac{1}{4}$yd (2.9m)
    Sizes 14, 16: 3$\frac{3}{8}$yd (3m)

Sizes 18, 20: 3$\frac{5}{8}$yd (3.3m)
45in (115cm)-wide fabric without nap:
    Sizes 10-14: 2$\frac{7}{8}$yd (2.6m)
    Sizes 16-20: 3$\frac{1}{8}$yd (2.8m)
36in (90cm)-wide lightweight interfacing: For all sizes: $\frac{1}{4}$yd (.2m)
Matching thread; 7in (18cm) skirt zipper; four 1in (2.5cm) buttons
Snaps; yarn for couched motif
Seam binding for hem

Note Embroidery can be worked before assembling or when garment is complete.

Key to adjusted pattern pieces
A	Back bodice	Cut 2
B	Back skirt	Cut 2
C	Front bodice	Cut 1 on fold
D	Front skirt	Cut 2
E	Back facing	Cut 2

F Front facing   Cut 1 on fold
Interfacing: use piece A (interface back opening only).

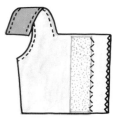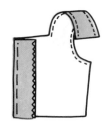

1 Staystitch the front and back neck and armhole edges of bodice and facings.

2 Baste the interfacing to the wrong side of the back bodice, matching one edge of facing to foldline down bodice. Catch-stitch in place. Finish center back edges. Turn center back facings to inside along foldline. Baste and press.

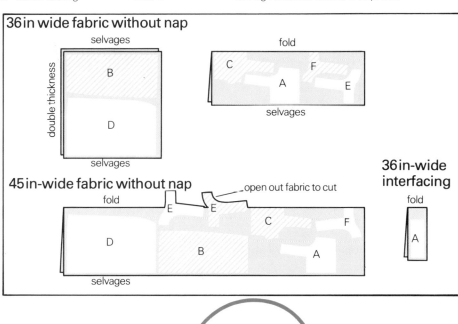

36in wide fabric without nap

45in-wide fabric without nap

36in-wide interfacing

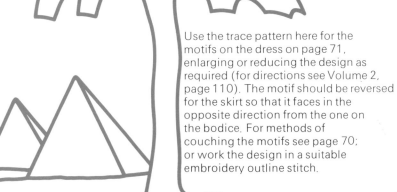

Brian Mayor

Use the trace pattern here for the motifs on the dress on page 71, enlarging or reducing the design as required (for directions see Volume 2, page 110). The motif should be reversed for the skirt so that it faces in the opposite direction from the one on the bodice. For methods of couching the motifs see page 70; or work the design in a suitable embroidery outline stitch.

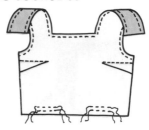

3 Fold, baste and stitch the front bust darts. Press darts downward. Run two rows of gathering across lower edges of front and back bodices, between the marks indicated on the pattern.

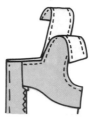

4 With right sides together, pin, baste and stitch end of back neck and armhole facing to center back facing as shown, taking a $\frac{3}{8}$in (1cm) seam allowance.
5 Join side seams of bodice and facings, attach facings, understitch and complete as described for one-piece facing on page 69.
6 Fold, baste and stitch the back waist darts of the skirt. Press darts toward center back. With right sides together, pin, baste and stitch the center back seam, leaving the opening for the zipper as indicated. Finish seam allowances and press them open.
7 Insert zipper in center back skirt opening. Press.
8 Fold the front tucks on the skirt into place and baste. Press. Finish the lower and front edges of the two skirt pieces by overcasting or zig-zag stitching. Press.
9 At lower edge of skirt fronts, trim away 1in (2.5cm) of hem allowance for 1$\frac{1}{4}$in (3cm) along front edges, leaving a $\frac{5}{8}$in (1.5cm) hem allowance as shown, to reduce bulk.

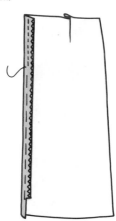

10 On right front, fold facing to wrong side baste to within 4in (10cm) of hem. Stitch to hip, $\frac{1}{4}$in (5mm) from edge.

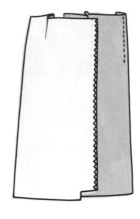

11 On the left front, fold facing to wrong side and press. Open it out and, using foldline as guide, overlay left to right front with right sides together, matching foldline to inner tuck line. Pin facing only along waistline to hold.

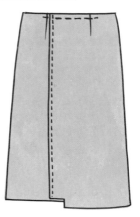

12 Fold back left front and press in place. Working from the right side, topstitch $\frac{1}{4}$in (5mm) in from the folded edge from waist to end of stitching. Baste facing down to within 4in (10cm) of hem. Baste right and left fronts together between tucks.
13 With right sides together and raw edges matching, pin, baste and stitch side seams. Finish seam allowances and press seams open.

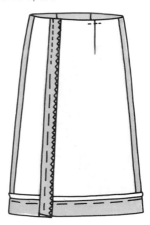

14 Open facings out and finish hem with seam binding, turn up and baste. Fold back facings; extend basting to hold.

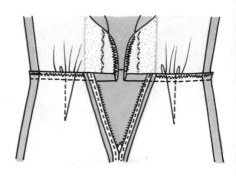

15 With right sides together and center fronts, side seams and center backs matching, pin the bodice to the skirt at the waistline, pulling up gathers to fit. Baste in place, spreading gathers evenly. Stitch waist seam. Trim seam allowance and overcast raw edges together. Press seam allowance upward.

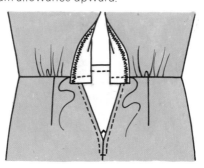

16 At waistline at center back, fold facing to right side. Pin, baste and stitch across bottom edge of bodice from edge of facing to center back. Clip corner and turn right side out. Press.

17 Complete hem using a suitable method. Complete topstitching at front edges of right and left fronts from hip to hem, $\frac{1}{4}$in (5mm) from the edges.
18 Make four horizontal buttonholes on right back bodice. Sew buttons and snaps in place at center back.

Shoestring

Night flights

Decorate plain sheets and pillowcases with bright balloon appliqué motifs — or any other motifs of your choice.

Materials
*Cotton-polyester sheet and
    pillowcase*
*Scraps of cotton-polyester fabric
    in several colours*
Thread to match motifs
Buttonhole twist to match sheet
Paper for pattern(s)
Dressmaker's marking pencil

1 Transfer the balloon pattern onto the paper. (Other motifs could be traced from a book or magazine — or, of course, drawn free-hand.)

2 Pin the pattern to the fabric and cut out the motif in the chosen colours.

3 Pin and baste the motifs to the sheet in the desired positions.

4 Using matching thread and a close zigzag stitch, work around the raw edges. Tie the thread ends on the wrong side.

5 Draw the balloon strings on the sheet, using the dressmaker's pencil.

6 Thread the machine with buttonhole twist and work over the drawn lines with a medium-to-long straight stitch.

7 Apply the motifs to the pillowcase in the same way, first ripping out one seam to facilitate the work.

8 Re-join the opened seam of the pillow case.

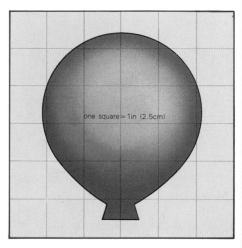

one square = 1in (2.5cm)

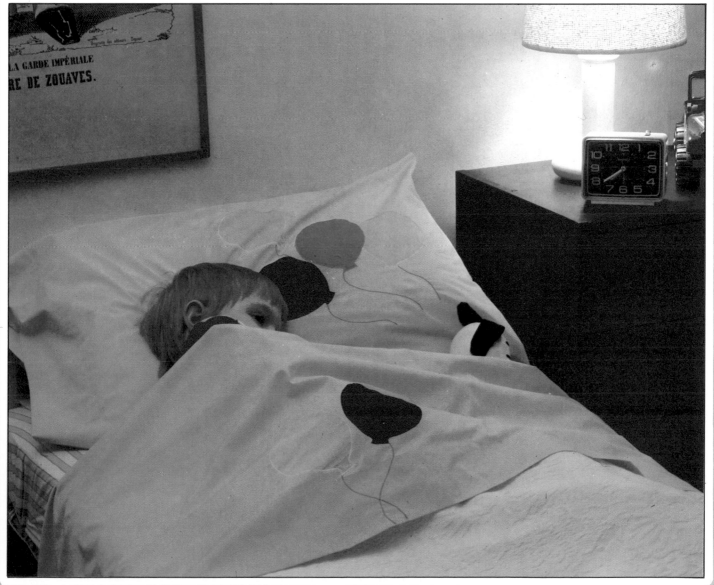

*Working with fabrics that
  ravel
*Padded tucks
*Pattern for an unlined coat;
  adapting the pattern;
  directions for making

Working with fabrics that ravel

Fabrics that ravel easily need careful handling and finishing on seam, hem and facing edges. Handle the fabric as little as possible during the construction of the garment. If it ravels a great deal, it may be advisable to zigzag around all cut edges before starting to assemble the garment. When cutting out, leave larger seam allowances than usual to allow for raveling if possible.

Staystitch any inner corners or clipped edges before sewing; also staystitch any seams that are likely to be put under stress. Reinforce yokes by mounting them onto the lining and then handling them as a single piece of fabric. The lining will strengthen the seams.

Seams that will be under stress, such as armholes, should be double-stitched. Although seams, hems and the raw edges of facings can be finished with zigzag stitch, this still does not completely prevent the fabric ends from raveling and it can look very untidy. A better method is to bind the seams, hems and facing edges with bias binding. On finer fabrics, French seams are ideal.

Padded tucks

Padded tucks give definition to a decorative tucked area. On the coat shown opposite, the tucks are planned to have a finished width of ⅜in (1cm) and are padded using the method described here. Any soft cord, yarn or foam strip is suitable for this method, as long as the padding material can be washed or dry-cleaned in the same way as the main fabric used for the garment.

An alternative method of padding the tucks, which will give a more raised and rounded effect, is to make the tuck with the filler cord inside, using a zipper foot on the machine. The stitching line will anchor the cord in place. Any size cord can be used, but the size of the tuck will vary accordingly, so this should be taken into account when adjusting the pattern for the tuck allowance, making it wider or narrower as desired.

1 Mark the tuck stitching lines on the wrong side with tailor's chalk or basting.

2 With the right side facing up, fold each tuck in place, matching the stitching lines. Baste. With the bulk of the fabric lying away from the tuck, stitch along the tuck stitching line to form the tuck. Press the tuck to one side.

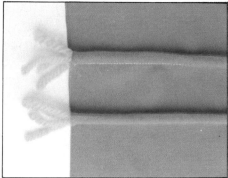

3 Cut pieces of yarn or cord to the length required to pad the tucks. Using a bodkin, thread the yarn or cord into the open end of the tuck and through the tuck to the other end.

Unlined coat

This simple coat is easy to make, as there is no lining to insert. It looks pretty over the sundress featured in the previous course.

Adapting the pattern
Measurements

The coat is adapted from the basic dress from the Pattern Pack, available in sizes 10 to 20, which correspond to sizes 8 to 18 in ready-made clothes.

Materials

*Four sheets of tracing paper 36in × 40in
  (90cm × 100cm approx)*
Flexible curve; yardstick; tracing wheel

1 Trace the dress pattern piece on paper, omitting the waist dart. Extend the grain line to top and bottom edges of pattern. To mark the straight center back edge, measure 1¾in (4.5cm) out from the grain line and draw the center back line from top to bottom edge of the pattern. Shorten the pattern by taking 10½in (27cm) off at the lower edge.

For the yoke line, measure down the center back edge from the back neck

cutting line: 7in (18cm) for sizes 10, 12; $7\frac{1}{2}$in (19cm) for sizes 14, 16; 8in (20cm) for sizes 18, 20; and draw a horizontal line across pattern, from center back to armhole edge. Draw a line through the center of the dart down to the yoke line. Drop the armhole at the side seam: first measure 1in (2.5cm) down the side seamline from the armhole cutting line; then, using a flexible curve, re-draw this part of the armhole curve, tapering the cutting line into original cutting line at the notches.

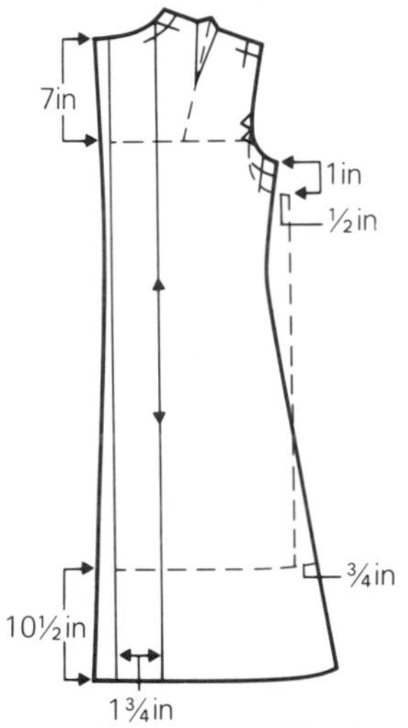

At the lower edge measure $\frac{3}{4}$in (2cm) in from the side cutting line and mark. At the side cutting line at the new armhole curve, add $\frac{1}{2}$in (1.3cm) and draw the new side cutting line from this point to the mark at the lower edge.

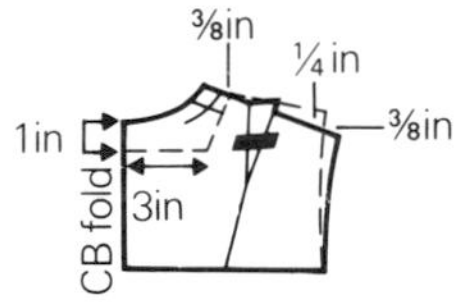

2 For the back yoke, trace the back yoke from the dress back pattern. Remove half the shoulder dart allowance at the armhole edge as shown, tapering into the original cutting line. Remove the remaining half of the dart allowance by folding half the dart away at the shoulder seam, tapering it to nothing at the bottom edge of the yoke. Tape it in place.
Raise the shoulder at the armhole edge by $\frac{1}{4}$in (5mm). Taper the new shoulder cutting line into the original cutting line at the neck edge.
For the new neckline measure 1in (2.5cm) down center back edge from the neck cutting line and draw a horizontal line across the pattern 3in (7.5cm) long for sizes 10, 12; $3\frac{1}{8}$in (8cm) for sizes 14, 16 and $3\frac{1}{4}$in (8.5cm) long for sizes 18, 20. Measure in $\frac{3}{8}$in (1cm) along shoulder seamline from the neck seamline and draw a diagonal line down to the horizontal line.

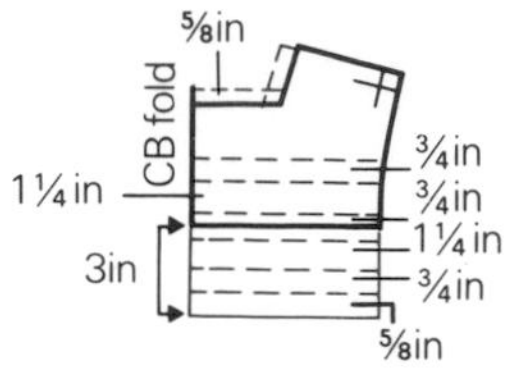

3 Add $\frac{5}{8}$in (1.5cm) seam allowance to new neck edges. Add 3in (7.5cm) to lower edge of yoke. Mark seamline at new lower edge. Beginning at seamline, draw parallel lines across pattern for tucks, measuring up $\frac{3}{4}$in (2cm), $1\frac{1}{4}$in (3cm), $\frac{3}{4}$in (2cm), $1\frac{1}{4}$in (3cm) and $\frac{3}{4}$in (2cm). The $\frac{3}{4}$in (2cm) spaces represent tucks.

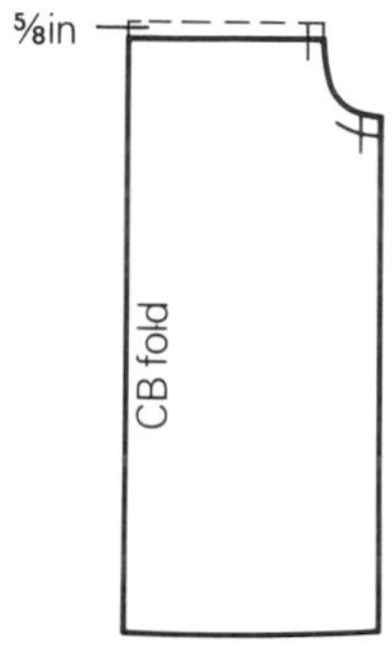

4 Trace the new back pattern. Add $\frac{5}{8}$in (1.5cm) seam allowance to the top edge. Mark the seam allowances. The center back is placed on a fold.
5 Trace the dress front pattern piece on paper, omitting the waist dart. Raise the shoulder line by $\frac{1}{4}$in (5mm) and drop the armhole 1in (2.5cm) as for the back. For the yoke line measure down the center front edge from the neck cutting line; $5\frac{1}{4}$in (13cm) for sizes 10, 12; $5\frac{1}{2}$in (14cm) for sizes 14, 16; $5\frac{3}{4}$in (15cm) for 18, 20.

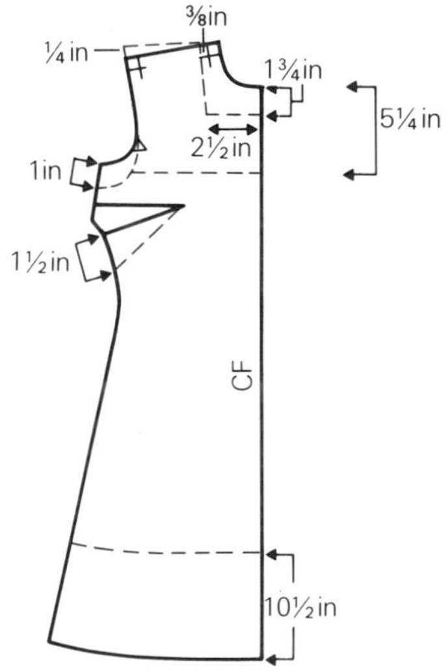

For the neckline measure $1\frac{3}{4}$in (4.5cm) down the center front from the neck cutting line and draw a horizontal line across the pattern; $2\frac{1}{2}$in (6.5cm) long for sizes 10, 12; $2\frac{3}{4}$in (7cm) for sizes 14, 16 and 3in (7.5cm) for sizes 18, 20. Measure $\frac{3}{8}$in (1cm) in along shoulder seamline from neck seamline, and draw a line from this point to the horizontal line as shown. Shorten the pattern at the lower edge by $10\frac{1}{2}$in (27cm).
Change the angle of the bust dart by measuring $1\frac{1}{2}$in (4cm) down side seam from the lower dart line; draw a line from this point to the dart point.

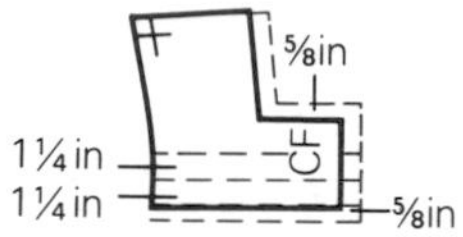

6 For the front yoke, trace the yoke shape from the front pattern.
Add $\frac{5}{8}$in (1.5cm) seam allowance to new neck edges, front edge and lower edge of yoke. Because of the sharper front armhole curve it is necessary to add the tuck allowance to the pattern by first cutting across the pattern and then inserting it. Beginning at lower edge, mark in the three tuck positioning lines, $\frac{5}{8}$in (1.5cm), $1\frac{1}{4}$in (3cm) and a further $1\frac{1}{4}$in (3cm). (Seamline is first tuck line.)

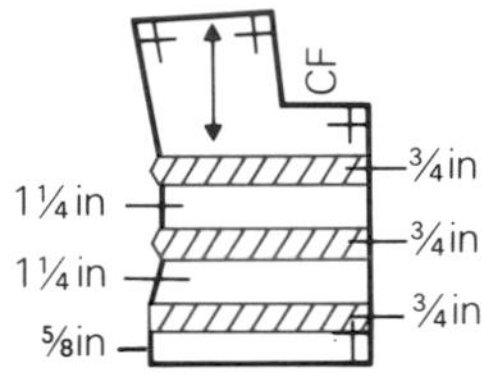

7 Cut along the three lines and insert a piece of paper $\frac{3}{4}$in (2cm) wide between each opening. This is for tuck allowance. Each cut edge represents a tuck seamline. To shape the armhole edge of the tucks, fold each tuck in place, folding downward. Cut along the armhole cutting line. Open out the tucks to see the shaping. Mark the grain line parallel to the center front edge. There will be $1\frac{1}{4}$in (3cm) spacing between the tucks.

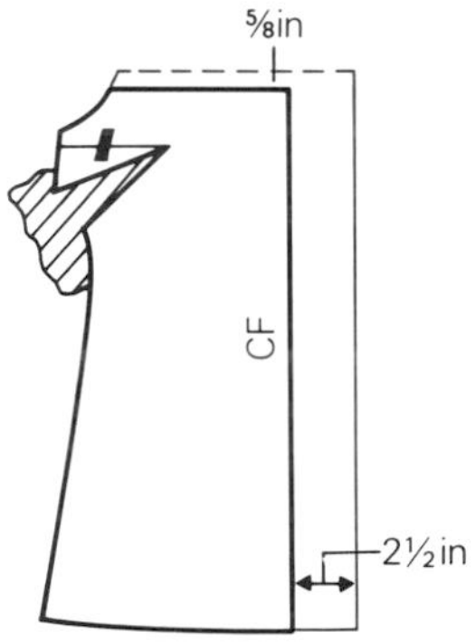

8 Trace the front pattern, allowing extra paper at the side and center front edges. Add $\frac{5}{8}$in (1.5cm) seam allowances to the top edge and $2\frac{1}{2}$in (6.5cm) to front edge for the facing. Cut along the new dart line, close the original dart and tape it in place. This will open the pattern at the new position. Insert and tape paper behind the opening.

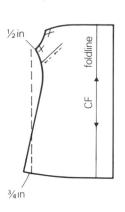

9 Fold the new dart in place and pin. At the lower edge measure $\frac{3}{4}$in (2cm) in from side cutting line. Add $\frac{1}{2}$in (1.3cm) at the side cutting line at new armhole curve, and draw the new side cutting line from the armhole curve to the mark at the lower edge. Using a tracing wheel, mark the cutting line at the dart position.

12 For the front neck facing, lay a piece of tracing paper over the front yoke and trace the cutting line of the neck and front edges and the lower edge and 3in (7.5cm) along shoulder cutting line. Draw the outline of the facing from the shoulder to the lower edge, keeping the width 3in (7.5cm), as shown. Mark the grain line parallel to the center front.

curve position on each side. Draw the new underarm cutting lines down to the lower edge, parallel to the grain line. Raise the seamline $\frac{1}{4}$in (5mm) at the center of the sleeve cap. Redraw sleeve cap seamline from center to new underarm seam. Draw a horizontal line from one underarm point to the other.

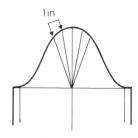

17 Mark five tuck positions around the sleeve head at 1in (2.5cm) intervals, placing the first in the center and two on each side. Draw slash lines from each tuck position to the center of the sleeve.

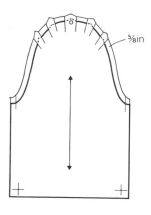

13 To make the pocket pattern, draw the shape of the pocket on the front pattern piece as shown, using a flexible curve. The pocket should be $7\frac{1}{2}$in (19cm) deep and slant downward.

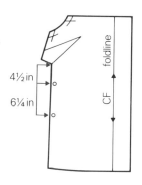

10 Open out the dart to see the shaping and draw the cutting line of the dart. Mark the seam allowances.
The center front is the straight grain and forms the foldline for the facing. To mark the pocket position on the side seamline, measure $4\frac{1}{2}$in (11cm) below bottom dart line for the top and then a further $6\frac{1}{4}$in (16cm) down for bottom. Mark the pocket position on the back pattern piece in the same way, taking the measurements from the front.

14 Trace the pocket shape. Mark the grain line parallel to center front of the garment. Add $\frac{5}{8}$in (1.5cm) seam allowance all around curved edge.

15 To make the sleeve pattern, trace the dress sleeve pattern piece. Extend the grain line to the top and bottom edges of the pattern.
To make the sleeve cap larger to fit the enlarged armhole, drop the underarm curve by measuring 1in (2.5cm) down underarm seamline from the cutting line of the curve on front and back edges of the sleeve.

18 Lay the pattern over a piece of paper ready to tape it in place. Cut along the slash lines from the top of sleeve cap then across to the side edges. Spread the top of each tuck $\frac{3}{4}$in (2cm), raising the section approximately $1\frac{3}{4}$in (4.5cm). Tape in place.

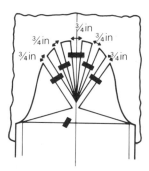

11 For the back neck facing, lay a piece of tracing paper over the back yoke. Trace the outline of the neck edge and 3in (7.5cm) along the center back edge and shoulder cutting line. Draw the outline of the back neck facing as shown.

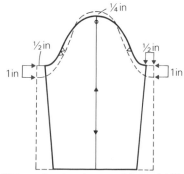

16 To make the sleeve wider, add $\frac{1}{2}$in (1.3cm) to the underarm edge at the new

19 Fold each tuck in place, folding the center and front tucks toward the front edge of the sleeve and the back tucks toward the back edge of sleeve. Using a tracing wheel, mark the top edge of each tuck. Open out tucks to see the shaping. Add $\frac{5}{8}$in (1.5cm) seam allowance to sleeve cap. A $\frac{3}{4}$in (2cm) hem is included at the lower edge.

Brian Mayor

Directions for making

Suggested fabrics

Linen, linen blends, lightweight woolens, medium-weight cottons and blends. Solid colors are preferable to prints, although thin stripes are suitable.

Materials

36in (90cm)-wide fabric with or without nap:
 Sizes 10 to 12: 3¾yd (3.4m)
 Sizes 14 to 16: 3⅞yd (3.5m)
 Sizes 18 to 20: 4yd (3.6m)
45in (115cm)-wide fabric with or without nap:
 Sizes 10 to 12: 3yd (2.7m)
 Sizes 14 to 16: 3⅛yd (2.8m)
 Sizes 18 to 20: 3⅓yd (3m)
36in (90cm)-wide interfacing:
 For all sizes: ½yd (.4m)
 13yd (12m) bias binding
Matching thread
Three ⅜in (1cm)-diameter buttons
Length of yarn or cord for tucks
Two shoulder pads

Key to adjusted pieces

A	Coat back	Cut 1 on fold
B	Back yoke	Cut 1 on fold
C	Coat front	Cut 2
D	Front yoke	Cut 2
E	Back neck facing	Cut 1 on fold
F	Front neck facing	Cut 2
G	Pocket bag	Cut 4
H	Sleeve	Cut 2

Interfacing: use pieces **C**, cut as shown, **E** and **F**. Cut as for facings.

1 Staystitch the inner corners of the front and back neck edges of yokes and facings. Mark the tuck lines with tailor's chalk or basting.

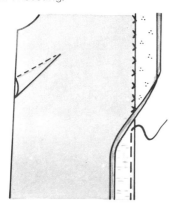

2 Baste interfacing to wrong side of the coat front facings. Catch-stitch the

interfacing to the fold line. Turn the front facings to the inside along fold line and baste close to folded edge. Press. Bind the outer edge of facings with bias binding to finish them.
3 Fold, baste and stitch the bust darts. Press darts downward.

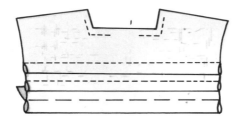

4 Make three padded tucks on front and back yokes (see page 76.) The bottom tuck on each yoke will be stitched when yokes are joined to main pieces and should only be basted at this stage. Press seam allowance at lower edge upward.

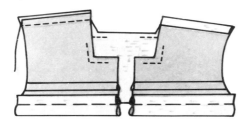

5 With right sides together, baste and stitch the shoulder seams. Finish and press the seams open.

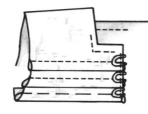

6 Make three tubing loops to fit around the button being used. Working on the right side, baste each loop to the center front edge of the right yoke — the top loop at the neck edge and the bottom loop above the yoke seam and the third between these two above the tuck.

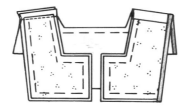

7 Baste the interfacing to the wrong side of the front and back neck facings. With right sides together, baste and stitch the facings together at the shoulder seams. Trim the interfacing close to the stitching. Finish and press seams open. Bind the outer edges of the neck facings to finish them.

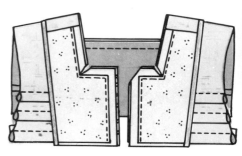

8 With the bottom seam allowance of yokes pressed upward and the tucks pressed downward and with right sides together and center fronts, shoulder seams and center backs matching, baste and stitch the front and back neck facing to the neck and front edges of yokes, catching in the button loops at the same time. Trim the seam allowances, trimming the interfacing close to the stitching, and clip into corners. Cut diagonally across the front corners. A ¼in (5mm) seam allowance will be left at bottom edge of front yoke facings.
9 Press the seam allowances toward the facings and understitch.

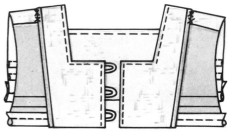

10 Turn the facings to the inside and baste around the neck edge. Press. Catch-stitch the facings to the shoulder seams.

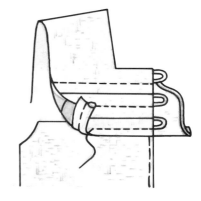

11 Open out the front facing at the bottom edge of the front yokes. With right sides together and center fronts and center backs matching, lap the yokes over the coat backs and fronts, matching the horizontal seamlines, and with the bottom tucks pressed downward and both seam allowances on the inside pressed upward. Baste and stitch from the right side along the tuck stitching lines, through all thicknesses. This will form the bottom tucks, as well as joining the yokes to the main coat pieces.

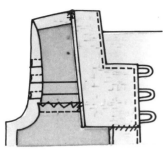

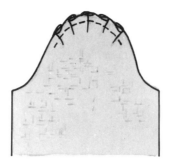

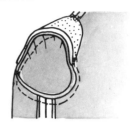

and shoulder points matching, pin and baste sleeve into armhole. Stitch seam.
21 Trim the seam allowance and clip the curved edges. Finish the seam allowances together with bias binding. Press seam toward sleeve. Repeat for second sleeve.

12 On the inside trim the yoke seams and overcast or zigzag stitch them together to finish. Turn under the $\frac{1}{4}$in (5mm) seam allowance at the bottom edge of the front yoke facings and then tack the facings to the front facing and the yoke seam allowance. Remove basting.

13 With right sides together, baste and stitch the pocket pieces to the back and front side seam edges at the positions marked.

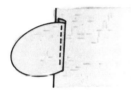

14 Press the seams toward the pockets and understitch

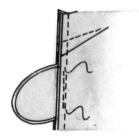

15 With right sides together, baste and stitch the side seams, stitching up to top and bottom edges of pockets. Finish the seam allowances with binding and press them open.

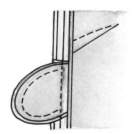

16 With right sides together, baste and stitch around the curved edge of the pockets. Finish them with bias binding.

17 Fold, pin and baste the tucks around the sleeve cap in place, folding the center and front tucks toward the front and the back tucks toward the back Press.
18 With right sides together baste and stitch the underarm seam of sleeves. Finish with bias binding.

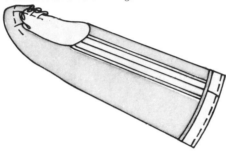

19 Finish the lower edge of the sleeve with bias binding. Turn the sleeve hems inside and baste close to the folded edge. Hem sleeves along bias binding.
20 With right sides together and seams

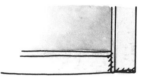

22 Make two shoulder pads as described in Volume 9, page 60. Sew pads to inside edge of shoulders.
23 Try on the coat and mark the hem. Turn the front facings out at the lower edge and turn the hem up. Baste close to the folded edge. Press. Finish the raw edge of the hem with bias binding and hem the coat.

24 Turn the front facing to the inside and slip stitch to the hem allowance. Press.
25 Sew the buttons on the front edge of the left yoke matching button loops.

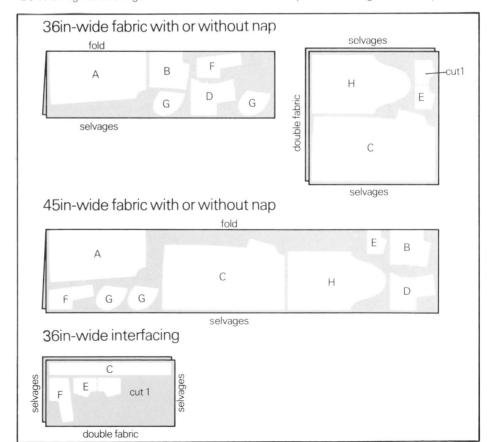

Needlework / COURSE 22

* Traditional crewelwork
* Long and short stitch
* Couching
* Shaded crossbar filling
* A crewel-embroidered box

Traditional crewelwork

Crewelwork, introduced in Needlework course 6, is basically free-style embroidery worked in wool. More specifically, the term refers to the elaborate, highly stylized embroideries worked in Britain and America during the 17th and 18th centuries.

Many of the traditional designs have an Oriental flavor—a reflection of the increased trade with Asia during this period. In the American Colonies, as well as in England, large crewel embroideries often featured the "Tree of Life," a design based on the Indian symbol of a tree as the creative force in the universe. The tree bears a profusion of different flowers, fruit and leaves on its gracefully winding branches. This fanciful assortment of blossoms is also typical of smaller crewel embroideries—such as the lid of the box pictured opposite, a modern piece of crewel work.

You can have great fun designing your own crewelwork, devising flowers that never grow on earth and arranging them in ingenious patterns. Begin by studying old embroideries in books and museums. Make tracings of photographs of flowers, simplifying them and selecting appropriate and novel stitches in which to interpret them.

At the same time, practice your stitching. Crewelwork demands excellent technique—a sure command of the needle.

Long and short stitch

Considerable practice is needed before this stitch can be worked effectively. It is used most often to create subtle effects of shading on petals, leaves and other objects. Colors may be shaded from dark to light or vice versa. In most cases the area to be filled has curved sides, so that the stitches must be slanted toward the center. First practice working the stitch in straight lines to fill a rectangle.

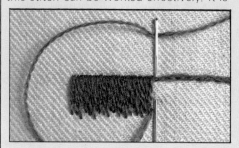

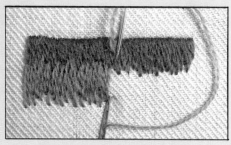

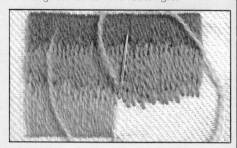

1 To produce a neat edge, first work split stitch (see Volume 5, page 77) along the top edge. Work the first row: bring the needle up about ½in (.1.3cm) below the edge and take it down just over the split stitch. Next, work another stitch close to the first one, but about ⅜in (1cm) long. Continue across the row, varying the length of the stitches rather freely, as shown.

2 To work the next row, bring the needle up through each stitch in the top row, splitting the thread, and take it down a short distance below. All the stitches in this row (and other intermediate rows) are about the same length; the uneven effect is maintained by working the same distance into each preceding stitch (about one-fourth of its length).

3 The bottom row is worked like the preceding intermediate row(s), except that the lower ends of the stitches follow the line of the area to be filled.

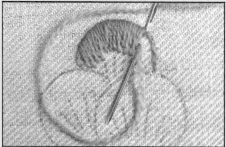

4 Before working long and short in a curved area, draw guidelines, in pencil or waterproof pen, to show the direction of the stitches. Then work split stitch along the edges. When working overlapping petals, complete the lower petals before working split stitch on overlapping edges.

5 Work the top row of long and short stitches, following the guidelines. The stitches must be placed very slightly farther apart on the edge than they are in the middle, in order to fan outward as required—without, however, leaving any gaps on the edge.

6 Subsequent rows are worked essentially the same as in step 2 above, but because of the curved shape they are likely to be somewhat more irregular. You will also find that it is not possible to work into every stitch in the preceding row. Practice to achieve a smooth effect.

Ray Duns

Couching

Couching is one of the most useful and versatile of embroidery stitches—as widely used in modern work as in traditional. It is basically very simple: one or more threads are applied to the fabric by means of small stitches taken over them, using either the same or contrasting threads. Couching may be used for lines or to fill spaces. It may be done in formal patterns or in a random way. In modern embroidery it is often used to apply thick novelty yarns to the fabric to create interesting textures.

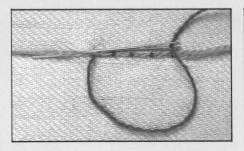

1 Lay the thread or threads to be couched on the stitching line, leaving a long end behind the starting point. With the couching thread work tiny stitches, about $\frac{1}{4}$in (5mm) apart, over the laid thread.

2 When the line of couching is complete, thread the free ends of the laid thread into a needle, take them to the wrong side and fasten off. To fill an area with couching, take the surface thread back and forth beside itself and work the couching stitches in a staggered pattern.

Shaded crossbar filling

Laidwork fillings are, in a sense, a variation of couching, since they involve taking threads across the fabric and then holding them in place with small stitches. The laid threads are taken to the wrong side at the edge of the motif, then brought to the right side at the same edge, rather than being taken back under to the opposite edge, as in satin stitch. They may cross the fabric in only one direction, or in two or more, but are always placed in a regular pattern. The tiny stitches worked over the top thread intersections hold the pattern in place. The samples at right show the shaded crossbar filling used for the box lid.

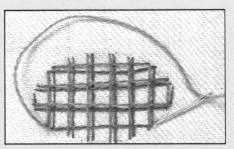

1 Begin by laying horizontal threads in the darkest of four shades at $\frac{1}{4}$in (5mm) intervals across the area to be filled. Cross these with vertical threads the same distance apart. Repeat, using a lighter shade each time and placing new threads above and to the left of the ones just laid.

2 When all four colors have been laid, they should cover the fabric completely in a basketweave pattern. Complete the filling by working tiny stitches in the lightest thread over the intersections of the top threads.

Imaginary garden

Subtle shades of rose and blue are combined in this graceful crewelwork design which decorates the lid of a jewel box.

Finished size 7¼×6×2¾in (18.5×15×7cm).

Materials

Piece of natural linen twill (or similar fabric) 12in (30cm) square
1 skein each of Appletons' crewel wool in the following colors: 321, 323, 325, 327 (dull marine blue range), 221, 223, 225, 227 (bright terracotta range)
Size 20 chenille needle, or medium-size crewel needle
Embroidery frame
Tracing paper
Dressmaker's carbon paper
Piece of ⅛in (2mm)-thick cardboard, 14×24in (36×61cm)
Piece of ⅜in (1cm)-thick foam, 22×7in (56×18cm)
¼yd (.2m) of 48in (122cm)-wide medium-weight upholstery fabric without nap
¼yd (.2m) of 48in (122cm)-wide medium-weight upholstery fabric,
such as moiré, for lining
Piece of light-colored felt, 14×5½in (35×14cm)
Fabric glue
Craft knife
Ruler
Right triangle
Matching thread
Strong thread, such as buttonhole twist
Curved surgical needle (optional)

Working the embroidery

1 Trace the design given on this page and transfer it to the linen using dressmaker's carbon paper.
2 Mount the fabric in the frame and work the embroidery, following the chart for colors and stitches and using one strand of thread throughout. Complete each motif before moving on to the next. As a general rule, you should work from bottom to top of a motif—that is, work the lower-lying petals, for example, before the overlapping ones. Below are

suggestions for working the individual motifs.
Upper right (1) outer row of satin stitch (see Volume 4, page 75) with needle taken down on outer edge; (2) inner row, with needle taken down on inner edge; (3) buttonhole stitch (see Volume 18, page 83) areas, with stitches slightly separated; (4) couched stem (page 83).
Lower right (1) top and bottom edges outlined in stem stitch (see Volume 4, page 75) in palest and darkest shades, respectively; (2) shapes filled with stem stitch in progressively dark/light shades, finishing with a line of palest shade along central stem.
Lower left (1) crossbar filling (see page 83); (2) long and short petals (see page 82) on each side of crossbar filling; (3) chain and stem stitch in edges of side petals; (4) French knots (see Volume 5, page 76) on side petals; (5) chain stitch (see Volume 18, page 83) around crossbar filling; (6) long and short and satin stitch buds (7) stem stitch stem.

KEY Dull marine blue 321, 323, 325, 327
Bright terracotta 221, 223, 225, 227

John Hutchinson

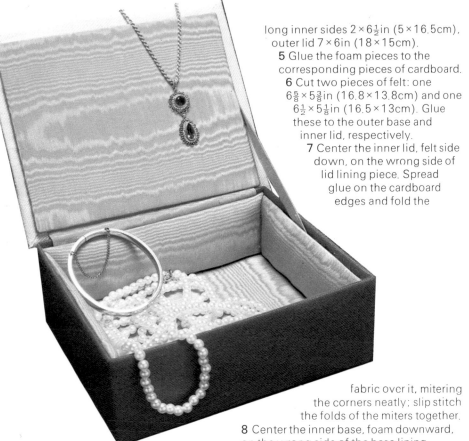

Upper left Long and short stitch working from lower petals back toward stem.
Main stem (1) back stitch (see Volume 5, page 76) on main stem; (2) couching and satin stitch leaves; (3) stem stitch on remaining stems.
3 Block the work as described in Volume 4, page 76. Leave the embroidery on the blocking board until you are ready to make the box.

Making the box

1 The box is constructed in two sections: an inner box and an outer one. Begin by cutting the following pieces from cardboard: inner box lid $6\frac{1}{2} \times 5\frac{1}{8}$in (16.5 × 13cm), base $6\frac{5}{8} \times 5\frac{3}{8}$in (16.8 × 13.8cm), 2 short sides $2 \times 5\frac{3}{8}$in (5 × 13.8cm), 2 long sides $2 \times 6\frac{1}{2}$in (5 × 16.5cm); outer box lid 7 × 6in (18 × 15cm), base $6\frac{5}{8} \times 5\frac{3}{8}$in (16.8 × 13.8cm), 2 short sides $2\frac{3}{8} \times 5\frac{1}{2}$in (6 × 14cm), 2 long sides $2\frac{3}{8} \times 6\frac{3}{4}$in (6 × 17cm). Measure and cut accurately, using the triangle for square corners and cutting with the craft knife held against the ruler.
2 Cut the fabric pieces for the outer box: base $8\frac{1}{2} \times 7$in (22 × 19cm), strip for sides $25\frac{1}{4} \times 4$in (64 × 10cm).
3 Cut the lining fabric pieces for the inner box: lid $8\frac{1}{2} \times 7$in (22 × 18cm), base $9\frac{1}{2} \times 8$in (24 × 20cm), 2 short sides 3 × $6\frac{3}{4}$in (8 × 17cm), 2 long sides 3 × 8in (8 × 20cm), hinge 12 × 2in (31 × 5cm), stay $6\frac{1}{4} \times 1\frac{1}{4}$in (16 × 3cm).
4 Cut the following pieces from the foam: inner base $6\frac{5}{8} \times 5\frac{3}{8}$in (16.8 × 13.8cm), 2 short inner sides $2 \times 5\frac{3}{8}$in (5 × 13.8cm), 2

long inner sides $2 \times 6\frac{1}{2}$in (5 × 16.5cm), outer lid 7 × 6in (18 × 15cm).
5 Glue the foam pieces to the corresponding pieces of cardboard.
6 Cut two pieces of felt: one $6\frac{5}{8} \times 5\frac{3}{8}$in (16.8 × 13.8cm) and one $6\frac{1}{2} \times 5\frac{1}{8}$in (16.5 × 13cm). Glue these to the outer base and inner lid, respectively.
7 Center the inner lid, felt side down, on the wrong side of lid lining piece. Spread glue on the cardboard edges and fold the fabric over it, mitering the corners neatly; slip stitch the folds of the miters together.
8 Center the inner base, foam downward, on the wrong side of the base lining piece. Keeping the foam compressed, glue the fabric edges over the cardboard (there is no need to miter the corners). Keep a weight on the base until the glue has dried.
9 Repeat step 8 to cover the four inner sides, gluing the short edges first, then the long ones. When the pressure is removed from the foam it expands to produce a well-padded shape.
10 Repeat step 8 to cover the outer lid with the embroidery, making sure that the design is placed correctly, and mitering the corners. Slip stitch the folds at the corners neatly.
11 Pin, baste and stitch the short ends of the outer box side piece, taking $\frac{3}{8}$in (1cm) seam allowance. Press the seam open and turn strip right side out.

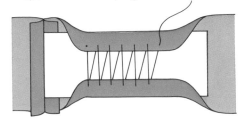

12 Place one of the shorter side pieces on the inside of the strip with one short edge at the seam. Using buttonhole twist, lace the fabric over the cardboard as shown, placing the stitches no more than $\frac{1}{4}$in (5mm) apart.
13 Add the remaining 3 sides, placing them end to end and alternating short with long, and continue lacing over them,

pulling the thread tight, but without breaking it or the fabric.
14 Center the outer base, felt side down, on the wrong side of the outer base fabric piece. Apply glue to the very edges of the cardboard only—not to the top or bottom—and press the fabric edges upward, so that they stick up straight. Cut away the fabric corners to reduce bulk.
15 Place the base inside the fabric-covered side piece and glue the fabric edges in place along the bottom.
16 Place the inner base inside the box, then insert the inner sides to check the fit. You may find it difficult to fit in the fourth side. If so, pull the fabric open at one end and trim away a small amount of cardboard and foam. Check the fit and re-glue the opened end.
17 Glue one long and one short inner side piece to the front and left sides of the box.
18 Press under $\frac{1}{4}$in (5mm) on each long side of the stay strip; then press the strip in half lengthwise, enclosing the raw edges. Slip stitch these edges together.

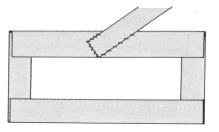

19 Pin one end of the stay to the remaining short inner side piece, a little less than halfway from the back, at an angle of about 35°. Tack it in place with a few stitches on each side, as shown.
20 Similarly fix the other end of the stay to one short side of the inner lid.
21 Press under $\frac{1}{4}$in (5mm) on the short ends of the hinge piece. Then press the strip in half crosswise. Slip stitch the folded edges together.
22 Apply glue to the underside of one long edge of the inner lid, to a depth of up to $\frac{3}{4}$in (2cm), and lay one long edge of the hinge on it. Allow glue to dry.
23 Glue the inner lid to the wrong side of the outer lid, enclosing the edge of the hinge, first making sure that the hinge is at the top of the embroidery. The inner lid should be slightly closer to the back of the box than to the front. Leave the lid under a weight until the glue has dried.
24 Glue the remaining free edge of the hinge to the inside back edge of the box, leaving a small gap between lid and box.
25 Glue the remaining inner side to the back of the box, over the hinge.
26 For additional strength, sew the base of the outer box to the sides, around the bottom. This can be done either invisibly, using a curved surgical needle, or with tiny cross stitches (see Volume 3, page 71) using a straight needle.

John Hutchinson

Bundle of joy

This beautiful christening gown is worthy of a memorable day. We've emphasized the delicate pure white crochet with pink ribbon and embroidery to produce an heirloom to treasure.

Sizes
To fit 18in (46cm) chest.
Length, 43in (109cm).

Materials
14oz (380g) of a sport yarn
Sizes C and E (3.00 and 3.50mm) crochet hooks
4 skeins stranded embroidery floss in random pink
2 skeins in random green
Medium-size tapestry needle
2¼yd (2m) of ⅜in (1cm)-wide ribbon
5 buttons; sewing thread

Gauge
22 sts and 20 rows to 4in (10cm) in bodice patt on Size C (3.00mm) hook.

Bodice
Using size C (3.00mm) hook make 28ch for center right back edge.
Base row 1sc into 2nd ch from hook, 1sc into each ch to end. Turn. 27sc.
Next row 1ch, 1sc into each sc to end. Turn.
Beg patt
1st row 4ch, skip first 2sc, *1dc into next sc, 1ch, skip next sc, rep from *to within last sc, 1dc into last sc. Turn. 13sps.
2nd row 1ch, 1sc into first dc, *1sc into next sp, 1sc into next dc, rep from *to within last 4ch, 1sc into last sp, 1sc into 3rd of 4ch. Turn.
3rd-5th rows 1ch, 1sc into each sc to end. Turn.
These 5 rows for the patt. Rep them twice more, then work the first to 3rd rows again.
Shape right armhole
Next row Patt across first 7sc, turn.
Next row Patt to end. Turn.
Next row 4ch, skip first 2sc, 1dc into next sc, (1ch, skip next sc, 1dc into next sc) twice, turn. 3sps.
Patt 2 rows, do not turn at end of last row but make 21ch. Turn.

Next row 1sc into 2nd ch from hook, 1sc into each of next 19ch, 1sc into each of last 7sc. Turn. 27sc.
Patt 9 rows.
Fasten off.
Shape neck
Next row Skip first 10 sts, rejoin yarn to next sc, 1sc into same place as joining, 1sc into each sc to end. Turn. 17sc.
Patt 19 rows, do not turn at end of last row but make 11ch. Turn.
Next row 1sc into 2nd ch from hook, 1sc into each of next 9ch, 1sc into each sc to end. Turn. 27sc.
Patt 9 rows.
Fasten off.
Shape left armhole
Next row Skip first 20sc, rejoin yarn to next sc, 1sc into same place as joining, 1sc into each of next 6sc. Turn. 7sc.
Patt 4 rows. 3sps.
Using a separate ball of yarn make 20ch and leave aside.
Next row 1ch, 1sc into each of the 7sc then work 1sc into each of the 20ch. Turn. 27sc.
Patt 19 rows.
Next row 4ch, skip first 2sc, 1sc into next sc, *1sc into each of next 3sc, 3ch, skip next sc, 1sc into next sc, rep from *3 times more, 1sc into each of last 4sc, do not turn but work 1sc into same place as last sc, 1sc into each row end along lower edge of bodice, turn.
Eyelet hole row 4ch, skip first 2sc, *1dc into next sc, 1ch, skip next sc, rep from * to last sc, 1dc into last sc. Turn.
Next row 1ch, 1sc into first dc, *1sc into next sp, 1sc into next dc, rep from * to within last sp, 1sc into last sp, 1 sc into 3rd of 4 ch.
Fasten off.

Sleeves
Join shoulder seams. Rejoin yarn to center of underarm and work 51sc evenly all around armhole. Turn.
Next row 3ch, *1dc into next sc, 2dc into

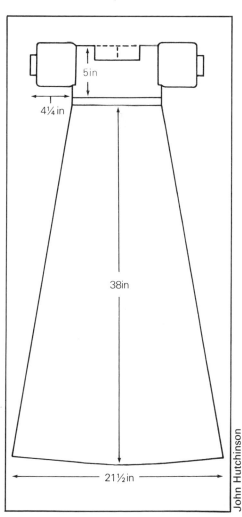

John Hutchinson

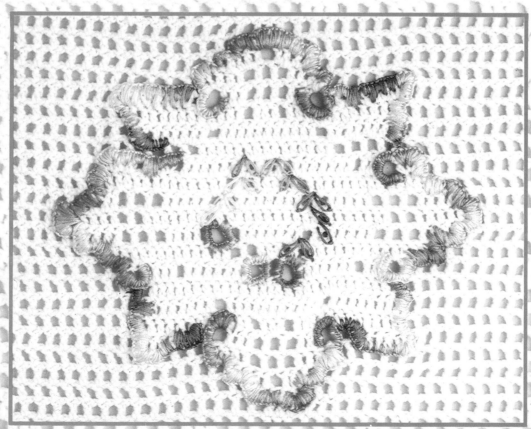

next sc, rep from * to end. Turn. 76 sts.
Next row 3ch, skip first dc, 1dc into each dc to end, 1dc into top of 3ch.
Rep last row 7 times more.
Next row 3ch, *work next 2dc tog – 1dc dec –, 1dc into next dc, rep from * to end. Turn. 51 sts.
Next row 1ch, *1sc into next dc, skip next dc, rep from * to end. Turn.
Next row 4ch, skip first 2sc, *1dc into next sc, 1ch, skip next sc, rep from * to last sc, finishing 1dc into last sc. Turn.
Next row 1ch, 1sc into each dc and sp to end. Turn.
Next row 1ch, *1sc into each of next 3sc, 3ch, sl st into last sc worked, rep from * to end.
Fasten off. Join underarm seam.

Skirt
Using size E (3.50mm) hook make 230ch.
Base row 1dc into 6th ch from hook, *skip next ch, 1ch, 1dc into next ch, rep from * to end. Turn. 113sps.
Reading RS rows from right to left and WS rows from left to right, cont in patt from chart 1 until 24 rows have been worked (ie 3 rows of diamonds).
Now foll chart 2, beg motif.
25th row As chart 2 to within 49th sp, work in diamond patt to end. Turn.
26th-64th rows Work in diamond and motif patt as set. Fasten off.

Make another piece in the same way.
Embroidery
Using all 6 strands of pink stranded embroidery floss work a close blanket stitch around four petals of each flower; then work in same way around each petal. Work close blanket stitch around 3 holes at center of each flower. Using green, work lazy daisy leaves to form a circle of leaves at center of each flower.

To finish
Join side seams of skirt. Work 1sc into each sp along top edge of skirt.
Next row 1ch, *1sc into each of next 2 sc, skip next sc, rep from * all around. Fasten off.
Using needle and thread attach skirt to bodice, matching underarms and side seams.
Along lower edge of skirt work 1sc into each dc and 1sc into each sp. Turn.
Picot row *1sc into each of next 3sc, 3ch, sl st to last sc, rep from * all around. Fasten off.

Neck edging
Work a row of sc around neck edge, turn and work picot row as for lower edge of skirt. Thread ribbon through the slots on front bodice (or front and back bodices if desired). Thread ribbon through waist slots and tie in bow at center front. Press work if appropriate for yarn used.

CHART 1

CHART 2 DIAMOND PATTERN

Technique tip

Blanket stitch

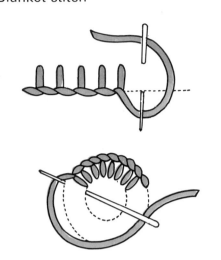

This stitch can be worked either close together to create a solid line (above), or slightly apart (above).
Secure yarn or thread on the wrong side of the work, bring needle and yarn to right side and insert needle in fabric for depth of stitch. Now make a straight downward stitch with the thread under the needle point. Pull up the stitch to form a loop. Continue in this way until the design is completed.

Lazy daisy stitch

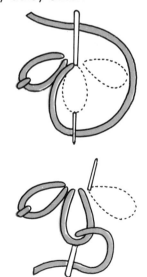

Secure yarn on the wrong side of the work, bring needle and yarn or thread to right side. Hold loop of yarn on right side with your thumb, then insert needle where it last emerged and bring it out a short distance from where it entered. Pull the yarn through, keeping the loop under the needle. Fasten the chain with a small stitch at the base of the loop. Continue in this way. Groups of lazy daisy stitches form the petals of flowers.

Terry Evans

Sweet dreams

These clever sleeping bags are ideal for a child to take along when spending the night with friends. When it's time to go, the bag can be picked up and transported home.

Sizes
Each bag measures 24×42in (61 × 107cm).

Materials
Knitting worsted
Loop stitch bag *31oz (875g)* in main
shade (A)
22oz (625g) of contrasting color (B)
Bag with surface crochet *37oz
(1000g)* in main shade (A)
2oz (50g) in each of 5 contrasting

Vince Loden

colors
Size K (7.00mm) crochet hook
*1½yd (1.3m) harmonizing fabric for
lining*

Gauge
9 sts and 6 rows to 4in (10cm) in dc
worked on size K (7.00mm) hook.

Loop stitch sleeping bag
Front
Using size K (7.00mm) hook and A, make
52ch.
Base row 1dc into 4th ch from hook, 1dc
into each ch to end. Turn. 50 sts.
Next row 3ch to count as first dc, skip
first dc, 1dc into each dc to end. Turn.
Rep last row 3 times more. Cut off A and
join in B. Beg loop and stripe patt.
1st row Using B, 1ch, (insert hook into
next st, wind yarn over index finger of
left hand 3 times, draw all loops through
st, yo and draw through all loops on hook,
give loops a gentle tug at back of work
to secure) — one loop st worked, make a
loop st into each st to end. Turn.
2nd row 1ch to count as first sc, 1sc
into each st to end.
Turn.
3rd row 1ch, 1 loop st into each st to end.
Turn.
4th row As 2nd.
5th-11th rows Work 3rd and 4th rows 3
times more, then rep 3rd row again.

Cut off B and join in A.
12th row Using A, 3ch, skip first st, 1dc into each st to end. Turn.
13th row 3ch, skip first dc, 1dc into each dc to end. Turn.
14th-16th rows As 13th.
Cut off A and join in B. Cont in patt as set until there are 5 stripes in B. Work 5 more rows in A. Fasten off.

Back
Work as for front until 5 rows have been completed. Rep last row until back measures same as front. Fasten off.

To finish
Using crochet as a pattern, cut 2 pieces of fabric for lining, leaving ½in (1cm) seam allowances all around.
Place 2 pieces of crochet with WS tog. Leaving an opening along one short edge and down to top of 2nd stripe in B, join 2 pieces tog by working in sc through both

thicknesses as foll: work 1sc into each row end of stripe in B, (1sc into next row end, 2sc into next row end) along dc row ends and working 3sc into each of the corners.
Fasten off.
Make lining to match bag, leaving slit in one side seam. Insert lining into bag with WS tog, turn under seam allowance and sew lining in position along top of bag and down opening.

Bag with surface crochet
Using size K (7.00mm) hook and A, make 52ch.
Base row 1dc into 4th ch from hook, 1dc into each ch to end. Turn. 50 sts.
Next row 3ch to count as first dc, skip first dc, 1dc into each dc to end. Turn. Rep last row until work measures 24in (61cm) from beg. Fasten off.
Make another piece in the same way.

Surface crochet
Using first contrasting color and keeping work very loose, work 1sc over 6th dc from long edge, now working parallel with long edge work (1sc into next dc, 2sc into next dc) to within 4 rows of end, work 3dc into next dc to turn, then working along the row, working over the tops of rows work 1sc into each dc to side edge. Fasten off. Using 2nd contrasting color, work in the same way as with first contrasting color, working the first section 6dc along and the 2nd section 4 rows apart from first contrasting color. Work rem contrasting colors in the same way, 6dc and 4 rows apart. After 5th contrast work 1 row first contrasting color and 1 row 2nd contrasting color.

To finish
Work as for loop stitch bag, leaving 12in (30cm) opening in side seam.

KNITTING

When vacations are approaching start your wardrobe with these tops designed to show off your tan. They're quick to make, so you can knit all four.

Sun tops

Tony Boase

Sizes

Beaded tube To fit 32-34in (83-87cm) bust. Length to underarm, 15¼in (39cm).
Top with contrasting borders To fit 32[34:36:38]in (83[87:92:97]cm) bust. Length to underarm, 13¾[13¾:14:14]in (35[35:36:36]cm).
Ribbed top with shaped detail Sizes as for top with contrasting border. Length at center front, 13[13½:14:14½]in (33[34:35:36]cm).
Cross-over top Sizes as for top with contrasting border. Length, 19½[20:20¾:21]in (50[51:53:54]cm).
Note Directions for larger sizes are in brackets [ ]; if there is only one set of figures it applies to all sizes.

Materials

Beaded tube *6oz (150g) of a sport yarn*
1 pair No. 3 (3¼mm) knitting needles
32 bugle beads and 32 round beads
Top with contrasting borders
4[4:6:6]oz (100[100:150:150]g) of a novelty sport-weight yarn in main shade (A)
2[2:4:4]oz (50[50:100:100]g) of contrasting color (B)
1 pair each Nos. 2 and 3 (2¾ and 3¼ mm) knitting needles
Ribbed top with shaped detail
6[6:7:8]oz (150[150:200:200]g) of a sport yarn
1 pair each Nos. 2 and 3 (2¾ and 3¼mm) knitting needles
Length of narrow elastic
Cross-over top *7[8:9:9]oz (200[200:250:250]g) of a novelty sport-weight yarn in main shade (A)*
2[2:4:4]oz (50[50:100:100]g) each in contrasting colors (B and C)
1 pair each Nos. 2 and 3 (2¾ and 3¼ mm) knitting needles; 2 buttons

Gauge

Beaded tube 44 sts and 34 rows to 4in (10cm) in ribbing on No. 3 (3¼mm) needles.
Top with contrasting borders 25 sts and 35 rows to 4in (10cm) in stockinette st on No. 3 (3¼mm) needles.
Ribbed top with shaped detail 30 sts and 38 rows to 4in (10cm) in stockinette st on No. 3 (3¼mm) needles.
Cross-over top 25 sts and 35 rows to 4in (10cm) in stockinette st on No. 3 (3¼mm) needles.

Beaded tube

To make

Using No. 3 (3¼mm) needles cast on 232 sts. Work 20in (51cm) K2, P2 ribbing. Bind off in ribbing.

Straps (make 2)

Using No. 3 (3¼mm) needles cast on 10sts.
1st row (RS) K2, *P2, K2, rep from * to end.
2nd row P2, *K2, P2, rep from * to end.
Rep last 2 rows for 10in (25cm). Bind off in ribbing.

To finish

Join back seam, reversing it for 4¾in (12cm) at top to turn back. Sew on bugle beads in groups of 4 on K sts of ribbing, with 2 rows between each bead of group. Attach first bead 8 sts from back seam and 12 rows from bottom edge of folded-down top. With 3 stripes of K ribbing between each group of 4 bugles, sew first bead of 2nd group of 4 bugles 6 rows up from last bead of first group. Rep these 2 groups 3 times more. Secure thread in bugle beads by threading it through a small round bead at the bottom. Sew on straps ½in (1cm) from top edge.

Top with contrasting borders

Front

**Using No. 2 (2¾mm) needles and B, cast on 88[94:102:108] sts.
1st row P1[2:2:1], K2, * P2, K2, rep from * to last 1[2:2:1] sts, P1 [2:2:1].
2nd row K1[2:2:1], P2, * K2, P2, rep from * to last 1[2:2:1] sts, K1[2:2:1].
Rep last 2 rows for 3½in (9cm); end with a first row. Cut off B. Join on A. Change to No. 3 (3¼mm) needles.
Next row P3[6:5:8], P into front and back of next st, * P8[8:9:9], P into front and back of next st, rep from * to last 3[6:6:9] sts, P to end. 98[104:112:118] sts. Cont in reverse stockinette st until work measures 12¼[12¼:12½:12½]in (31[31:32:32]cm); end with a K row. **

Shape top

1st row P to last 6[6:7:7] sts, turn.
2nd row Sl 1, K to last 6[6:7:7] sts, turn.
3rd row Sl 1, P to last 12[12:14:14] sts, turn.
4th row Sl 1, K to last 12[12:14:14] sts, turn. Cont to work 6[6:7:7] sts less on alternate rows in this way until 24[24:28:28] sts are left unworked at each side. Cut off yarn. Sl rem 24[24:28:28] sts onto same needle.

Border

Using No. 2 (2¾mm) needles, B and with RS of work facing, cont as foll:
1st row K6[6:7:7], pick up loop lying between needles and K tog with next st – called (M1) K2 tog –, (K5[5:6:6], [M1] K2 tog) 3 times, K49[55:55:61], * (M1) K2 tog, K5[5:6:6], rep from * to end.
2nd row K2[1:1:2], P2, *K2, P2, rep from * to last 2[1:1:2] sts, K2[1:1:2].
3rd row P2[1:1:2], K2, * P2, K2, rep from * to last 2[1:1:2] sts, P2[1:1:2].
Rep 2nd and 3rd rows 6 times more. Bind off in ribbing.

Back

Work as for front from ** to **. Cut off A. Join on B.

Border

Using No. 2 (2¾mm) needles and B, K1 row. Work 14 rows ribbing as for front border. Bind off in ribbing. Join side seams.

Ribbed top with shaped detail

Back

**Using No. 2 (2¾mm) needles cast on 115[121:129:137] sts.
1st row K1, *P1, K1, rep from * to end.
2nd row P1, *K1, P1, rep from * to end.
Rep last 2 rows for 2in (5cm); end with a first row.
Next row Rib 29[20:21:34], pick up loop lying between needles and K tbl—called make 1 (M1)—, (rib 57[40:43:68], M1), 1[2:2:1] times, rib to end. 117[124:132:139] sts. Change to No. 3 (3mm) needles. Beg patt.
1st row (RS) P0[1:0:1], *P2, K1, P1, K1, rep from * to last 2[3:2:3] sts, P2[3:2:3].
2nd row K0[1:0:1] * K2, P3, rep from * to last 2[3:2:3] sts, K2[3:2:3].
The last 2 rows form patt. Cont in patt until work measures 12½[13:13½:13¾]in (32[33:34:35]cm); end with a 2nd row and inc 0[1:1:0] st at center of last row. 117[125:133:139] sts. ** Change to No. 2 (2¾mm) needles. Work 15 rows K1, P1 ribbing. Bind off in ribbing.

Front

Work as for back from ** to **
Change to No. 2 (2¾mm) needles. Work 3 rows K1, P1 ribbing.
Next row Rib 58[62:66:69], M1, rib to end. 118[126:134:140] sts.
Insert a marker at each end of last row.
Shape left front flap
Next row Rib 59[63:67:70], turn and leave rem sts on a spare needle.
***Work 10 rows ribbing on these sts.
Next row Rib 49[52:55:59], turn.
Next row Sl 1, rib to end.
Next row Rib 39[41:44:46], turn.
Next row Sl 1, rib to end.
Next row Rib 29[30:33:34], turn.
Next row Sl 1, rib to end.
Next row Rib 9[10:11:11], turn.
Next row Sl 1, rib to end.
Bind off in ribbing. ***
Shape right front flap
Using No. 2 (2¾mm) needles and with RS of work facing, rejoin yarn and rib to end. Work 1 row. Complete as for left front flap from *** to ***

To finish

Do not press. Join side seams. Cut elastic to fit just above bust and join into a ring. Work herringbone casing over elastic.

Cross-over top

Left front

**Using No. 2 (2¾mm) needles and A, cast on 99[105:111:119] sts.
1st row K1, *P1, K1, rep from * to end.

2nd row P1, * K1, P1, rep from * to end.
Rep last 2 rows 6 times more, then work first row again.
Next row Rib 11[10:11:13], pick up loop lying between needles and K tbl—called make 1 (M1)—, (rib 19[21:22:23], M1) 4 times, rib to end. 104[110:116:124] sts. **
Change to No. 3 (3¼mm) needles. Beg with a K row, cont in stockinette st and stripe patt of 6 rows A, 2 rows B, 6 rows A and 2 rows C, **at the same time** shape front edge by dec one st at beg of every other row until 57[63:69:77] sts rem; end with a P row.
Shape armhole
Cont to shape at front edge as before, work armhole as foll:
Next row Bind off 3 sts, K to end.
Next row P2 tog, P to end.
Dec one st at armhole edge on next 5[7:5:7] rows, then on foll 5[5:9:9] alternate rows, **at the same time** cont to dec at front edge as before until 37[39:40:45] sts rem.
Keeping armhole edge straight, dec one st at front edge only as before until 19[20:20:22] sts rem.
Cont straight until armhole measures 7[7½:8¼:8½]in (18[19:21:22]cm); end with a P row.
Shape shoulders Bind off 10[10:10:11] sts at beg of next row. Work 1 row. Bind off 9[10:10:11] sts.

Right front

Using No. 2 (2¾mm) needles and A, cast on 99[105:111:119] sts.
Work 7 rows ribbing as for left front from ** to **
Next row (buttonhole row) Rib 2, bind off 3, rib 89[95:101:109], bind off 3, rib to end.
Next row Rib to end, casting on 3 sts over those bound off in previous row. Work a further 6 rows ribbing. Complete to match left front, reversing shaping.

Back

Work as for left front from ** to **
Change to No. 3 (3¼mm) needles. Beg with a K row, cont in stockinette st and stripe patt until back matches front to underarm; end with a P row.
Shape armholes
Bind off 3 sts at beg of next 2 rows.
Dec one st at each end of every row until 88[90:100:104] sts rem, then at each end of every foll alternate row until 78[80:82:86] sts rem.
Cont straight until back matches front to shoulder, ending with a P row.
Shape shoulders
Bind off 10[10:10:11] sts at beg of next 2 rows and 9[10:10:11] sts at beg of foll 2 rows. Bind off rem 40[40:44:44] sts.

Front border

Join shoulder seams. Using No. 2 (2¾mm) needles and C, cast on 4 sts.

Work in garter st until strip, slightly stretched, fits up front, around neck and down right front to lower edge. Bind off.

Armhole borders

Using No. 2 (2¾mm) needles and B, cast on 4 sts. Work in garter st until strip, slightly stretched, fits around armhole.

To finish

Do not press. Sew on borders. Join side seams. Sew on buttons.

Technique tip

Elastic casing

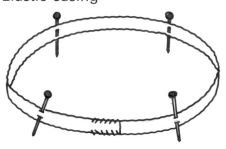

Cut a length of narrow elastic to fit snugly around the top of the bust, allowing ⅝in (1.5cm) to overlap. Sew elastic into a circle, securing the ends with a few strong stitches. Divide the circle into four equal parts and mark with pins.

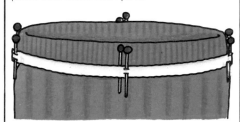

Divide the knitting into quarters around the upper edge at the casing position, and mark the elastic in place, matching the quarter section pins on the elastic with those on the knitting. Stretch the elastic slightly to fit.

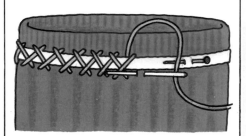

Thread a tapestry needle with a strand of matching yarn. (Contrasting yarn is shown here for clarity.) Secure yarn at casing position at left-hand side seam of knitting. Work herringbone stitch from left to right encasing the elastic as you work. Distribute the knitting evenly and finish off thread securely.

KNITTING

The simple cable stitch used on this man's vest can be worked without the use of a cable needle.

Mock cable classic

Size
To fit 40in (101cm) chest.
Length, 25in (64cm).

Materials
14oz (400g) of a knitting worsted weight yarn.
One pair each No.6 (4mm) and No. 10 (6mm) needles

Gauge
14 sts and 18 rows to 4in (10cm) in st st on No.10 (6mm) needles.

Back
Using No.6 (4mm) neeldes, cast on 78 sts.
Work in K1, P1 ribbing for 2½in (6cm) ending with a WS row.

Change to No.10 (6mm) needles and work in st st until back measures 16½in (42cm) from beg, ending with a WS row.
Shape armholes
Bind off 4 sts at beg of next 2 rows. Bind off 3 sts at beg of next 4 rows. Dec one st at each end of next row. 56 sts.
Work even until back measures 25in (64cm) from beg, ending with a WS row.
Shape shoulders
Bind off 8 sts at beg of next 2 rows.
Bind off 6 sts at beg of next 2 rows.
Bind off rem 28 sts.

Front
Work ribbing as for back, inc 6 sts evenly across last ribbing row. 84 sts.
Change to No.10 (6mm) needles and beg patt as foll:

1st row K16, *P1, K4, P1, K17, rep from * twice more, ending last rep K16 instead of K17.
2nd row K all K sts and P all P sts.
3rd row K16, * P1, T4F (K the 3rd and 4th sts on left-hand needle, leaving them on the needle, K the first and 2nd sts, sl all 4 sts off the needle tog), K17, rep from * twice more, ending last rep K16 instead of K17.
4th row As 2nd row.
5th row As first row.
6th row As 2nd row.
7th row As first row.
8th row as 2nd row.
3rd-8th rows form the patt.
Keeping patt correct, cont until front measures same as back to armhole shaping, ending with a WS row.
Shape armholes
Work armhole shaping as given for back 62 sts.
Keeping patt correct, work even for 2 rows.
Shape neck
Next row Work 29 sts, K2 tog, turn. Working on these sts only and keeping patt correct, dec one st at beg of next and every other row until 16 sts rem. Work on these 16 sts until front measures same as back to shoulder shaping, ending with a WS row.
Shape shoulder
Cast off 9 sts at beg of next row. Work one row. Bind off rem sts.
Shape second side of neck
Rejoin yarn to rem sts with RS of work facing. Work 2 tog, patt to end of row. Work as for first side of neck, reversing shaping.

Neckband
Join right shoulder seam. With RS of work facing and with No.6 (4mm) needles, pick up and K38 sts down left side of neck, pick up and K1 st from center (mark this st with a colored thread), pick up and K38 sts up right side of neck, pick up and K28 sts from back neck. 105 sts.
1st row (WS) Rib to within 2 sts of marked st, P2 tog, P1, P2 tog tbl, rib to end.
2nd row Rib to within 2 sts of marked st, P2 tog tbl, K1, P2 tog, rib to end.
Rep last 2 rows once, then first row again. Bind off in K.

Armbands
Join left shoulder seam.
With RS facing and using No.6 (4mm) needles, pick up K84 sts along armhole. Work in K1, P1 ribbing for 6 rows. Bind off in P.

To finish
Press according to instructions on the yarn label.
Join neckband seam.
Join side and armband seams.

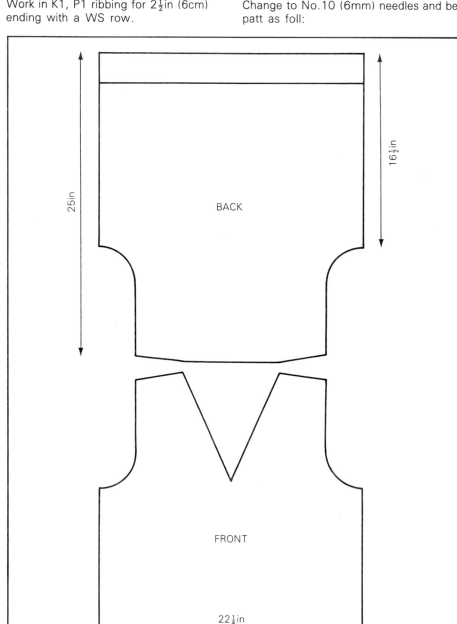

BACK

16½in

25in

FRONT

22¼in

2¼in

EXTRA SPECIAL SEWING

Stretch out in the sun

A slinky bathing suit to take to the sun. Add a harmonizing wraparound skirt for lunch or drinks by the pool.

Measurements
To fit sizes 10, 12 and 14.
Finished back length of skirt: 37½in (95cm).

Suggested fabrics
For the bathing suit; a two-way stretch knit. For the skirt: printed cotton.

Tony Boase

Bathing suit

Materials

- $\frac{7}{8}$yd (.8m) of 60in (150cm)-wide fabric
- $2\frac{1}{8}$yd (1.9m) of $\frac{1}{4}$in (5mm)-wide elastic
- $\frac{7}{8}$yd (.8m) of $\frac{1}{2}$in (1.3cm)-wide woven tape
- $1\frac{3}{4}$yd (1.5m) of thick cord
- Matching thread
- Yardstick, flexible curve
- Pencil, paper for pattern

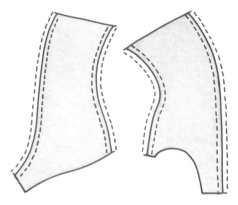

1 For an accurate fit it is advisable to make a paper pattern for each piece before cutting out, following the measurement diagrams.

Note Measurements given are for size 12. For size 10 cut away $\frac{1}{4}$in (5mm) from center front, center back and side seams. For size 14 add on $\frac{1}{4}$in (5mm) at center front, center back and side seams. Check the length of the bathing suit and adjust at waist if necessary before cutting out. Following the cutting layout, place the pattern pieces on the fabric, so that the grain lines follow the straight grain of the fabric.

Cut two fronts and two backs. Cut one crotch lining.

A $\frac{5}{8}$in (1.5cm) seam and hem allowance is included.

2 With right sides together, pin, baste and stitch fronts together at center front and backs together at center back. Finish the seam allowances.

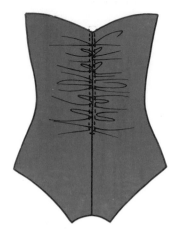

3 Run a row of gathers on each side of center front seam, extending 15in (38cm) from top edge. Pull up gathers to measure 10in (25cm) and fasten securely.

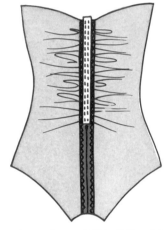

4 Cut a piece of tape $10\frac{1}{4}$in (26cm) long. On wrong side of bathing suit center the tape over gathers and baste it in place. Working from the right side, stitch through fabric and tape $\frac{1}{8}$in (3mm) away from seam on each side. Remove gathering stitches.

5 Repeat on bathing suit back.

6 Pin, baste and stitch front to back at side seams. Trim seam allowances to $\frac{1}{4}$in (5mm) and finish them together.

Finish upper, curved edge of crotch lining.

With right side of crotch lining facing wrong side of back, place straight edge of crotch lining even with lower edge of back and baste it in place.

Terry Evans

7 With right sides together, pin, baste, and stitch front to back at crotch seam. Trim seam and press crotch lining toward front. Baste to front around legs. Catch-stitch center of crotch lining to center front seam allowances. To form casing for leg elastic, turn under $\frac{1}{4}$in (5mm) and then $\frac{1}{2}$in (1.3cm) to wrong side around leg edges. Pin, baste and stitch close to first fold, leaving an opening for threading. Cut two pieces of elastic to fit top of thigh, plus $1\frac{1}{4}$in (3cm). Thread elastic through leg casings, overlap ends by $\frac{5}{8}$in (1.5cm) and stitch securely. Close openings in casing stitching.

Make casing for elastic around top of bathing suit in same way. Insert elastic and finish as for leg casings.

Cut a piece of tape 2in (5cm) long and attach it to wrong side of center front of bathing suit, just below finished top edge to form a loop. Thread cord through loop and knot ends. Tie cords behind neck or remove them for sunbathing.

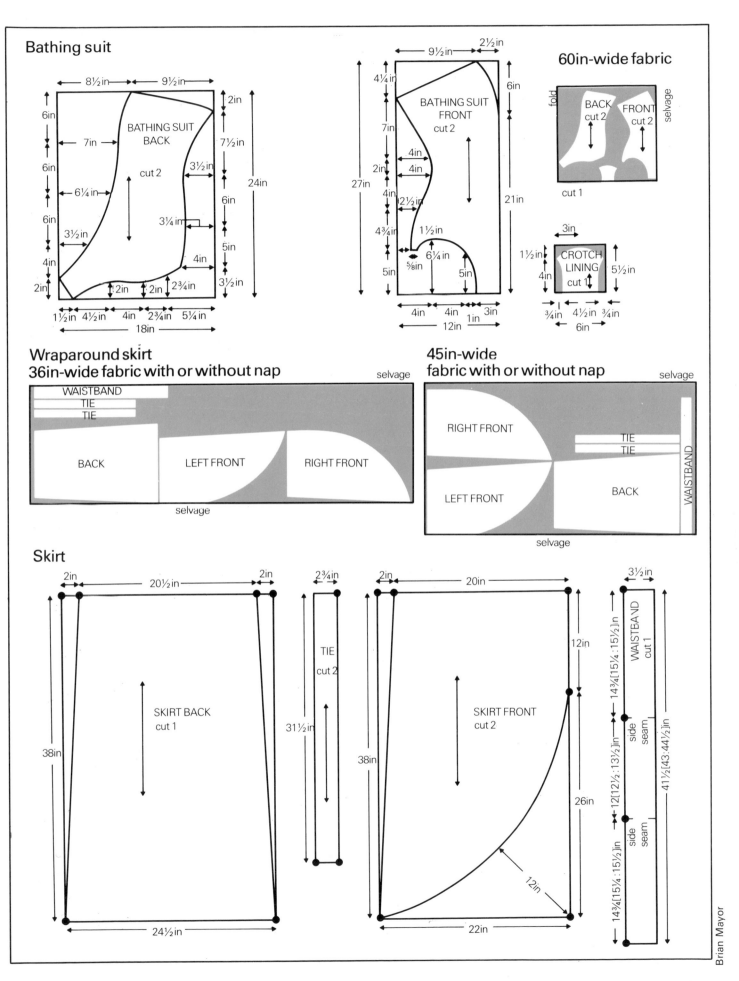

Bathing suit

BATHING SUIT BACK cut 2

8½in · 9½in · 2in · 6in · 7in · 7½in · 3½in · 6in · 6¼in · 24in · 6in · 3¼in · 6in · 3½in · 4in · 5in · 2in · 2in · 3½in · 4in · 2in · 3½in · 1½in · 4½in · 4in · 2¾in · 5¼in · 2¾in · 18in

BATHING SUIT FRONT cut 2

9½in · 2½in · 4¼in · 6in · 7in · 2in · 4in · 4in · 27in · 4in · 21in · 2½in · 4¾in · 1½in · ⅝in · 6¼in · 5in · 5in · 4in · 4in · 3in · 1in · 12in

60in-wide fabric

BACK cut 2 · FRONT cut 2 · fold · selvage · cut 1

CROTCH LINING cut 1

1½in · 3in · 4in · 5½in · ¾in · 4½in · ¾in · 6in

Wraparound skirt
36in-wide fabric with or without nap

selvage

WAISTBAND · TIE · TIE · BACK · LEFT FRONT · RIGHT FRONT

selvage

45in-wide fabric with or without nap

selvage

RIGHT FRONT · TIE · TIE · WAISTBAND · LEFT FRONT · BACK

selvage

Skirt

SKIRT BACK cut 1

2in · 20½in · 2in · 38in · 24½in

TIE cut 2

2¾in · 31½in

SKIRT FRONT cut 2

2in · 20in · 2in · 12in · 38in · 26in · 22in · 12in

WAISTBAND cut 1

3½in · 14¾[15¼ : 15½]in · 12[12½ : 13½]in · side seam · 41½[43 : 44½]in · side seam · 14¾[15¼ : 15½]in

Skirt

Materials

$3\frac{3}{8}$yd (3m) of 36in (90cm)-wide
fabric or $2\frac{1}{4}$yd (2m) of 45in (115
cm)-wide fabric (add $\frac{1}{2}$yd (.5m) for
matching large patterns)
4in (10cm) of 36in (90cm)-wide
interfacing
$3\frac{7}{8}$yd (3.5m) of $\frac{1}{2}$in (1.3cm)-wide
bias binding
Matching thread; tailor's chalk
Yardstick; flexible curve

1 Following diagram, draw measurements on fabric with chalk. Cut one back, two fronts, one waistband and two ties. Remember to cut the skirt front in reverse for left front. On both fronts draw a smooth curve at the lower edge, following the measurements given, and cut out.

Mark the side seam positions on the waistband with tailor's tacks. Cut interfacing for waistband, the same length and half the width.

Note Measurements are given for size 10. Figures for sizes 12 and 14 follow in brackets []. If only one figure is given, it applies to all sizes.

A $\frac{5}{8}$in (1.5cm) seam allowance is included, except where stated otherwise.

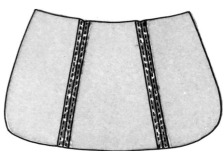

2 With right sides together, pin, baste and stitch the back to the fronts at the side seams. Press seams open and finish seam allowances.

Tony Boase

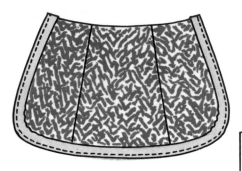

3 Open out one edge of the bias binding. With raw edges even and right sides together, pin, baste and stitch binding around side and lower edges of skirt. Press to the wrong side and slip stitch in place.

4 Add two rows of gathers around the upper edge of the skirt, leaving a $6\frac{1}{4}$in (16cm) gap unstitched at center of both fronts, so that front panels will lie flat.
5 Baste the interfacing to wrong side of waistband. With right sides together and interfacing along upper edge, pin the skirt to the waistband, matching the side seams to tailor's tacks on the waistband. Leave the ends of the waistband extending $\frac{5}{8}$in (1.5cm) beyond finished edges of the skirt. Pin the center of the skirt front and back to center of waistband front and back. Pull up gathers to fit waistband and distribute them evenly. Pin, baste and stitch skirt to waistband. Trim seam allowances and press them toward waistband. Press under a $\frac{5}{8}$in (1.5cm) seam allowance along remaining long edge of waistband.
6 With right sides together, fold ties in half lengthwise. Pin, baste and stitch along long edges and one short end. Trim seams. Turn right side out; press.

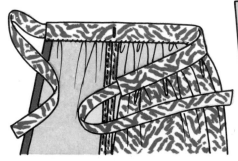

7 Pin ends of ties to right side of waistband, $\frac{1}{4}$in (5mm) above waist seam,

with raw edges even, and baste. With right sides together, fold waistband so that folded edge meets waist seam. Stitch across short ends. Trim seam allowances. Turn right side out and press. Pin and baste folded edge over seam. Hem in place. Make a hand- or machine-stitched buttonhole in the waistband

at the right side seam.
8 To put on the skirt: wrap the right front over the left. Bring the left tie out through the buttonhole opening in the waistband and bring the ends together to tie in a bow. The wraparound style makes this skirt perfect for a sun-and-sand vacation.

Technique tip

Working with stretch fabric

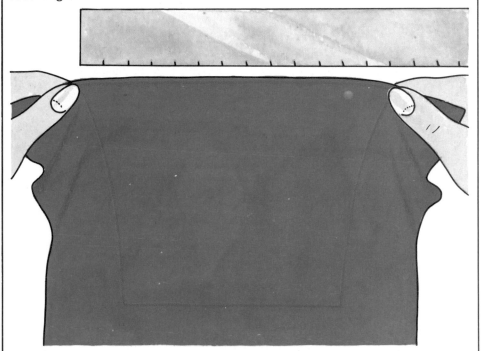

If a garment has been designed to be made in a stretch fabric, it has been cut with less ease allowance than is usual. Conventional fabrics should not be substituted or you will find that the garment will not fit. Before buying the full amount of fabric, buy a few inches to check that it has the amount of stretch required by the pattern.

For the bathing suit shown here, mark a 4in (10cm) square on the fabric. Use a ruler to make sure that the fabric will stretch to between 5in (13cm) and 6in (15cm) in both directions.

Ideally, all seams should be stitched with a special stretch stitch designed for stretch fabrics. Your machine manual should give details. Zig-zag stitch can be used as an alternative. It is possible to make the bathing suit with a straight stitch machine, but be sure to use a polyester thread and stretch the fabric slightly as you sew to give as much elasticity as possible to the seams.

Terry Evans

Luxury lingerie

A complete set of lingerie for real luxury: Make your own teddy, slip, nightgown and French panties, all trimmed with lace. All the garments are cut on the bias from the same basic pattern with a minimum of seams.

Measurements

To fit sizes 10[12:14:16].
Note Measurements are given for size 10. Measurements for larger sizes are given in brackets []. If only one figure is given, this applies to all sizes.

Suggested fabrics

Satin, sheer tricot.

Teddy

Materials

$1\frac{1}{8}$yd (1m) of 54in (140cm)-wide fabric or $1\frac{1}{2}[1\frac{5}{8}:1\frac{3}{4}:1\frac{7}{8}]$yd (1.3[1.4: 1.5:1.6]m) of 36in (90cm)-wide fabric
$1\frac{1}{2}$yd (1.3m) of lace for bodice
$1\frac{3}{4}$yd (1.5m) of lace for legs
Three $\frac{3}{8}$in (1cm)-diameter buttons or button forms
$3\frac{3}{8}$yd (3m) of $\frac{3}{8}$in (1cm)-wide satin ribbon for straps and waist tie
$1\frac{1}{4}$yd (1.1m) of $\frac{3}{4}$in (2cm)-wide ribbon for casing
Matching thread, yardstick, flexible curve, paper for pattern

1 Draw the pattern following the appropriate figures on the measurement diagram.
2 Prepare fabric and cut out, noting that the main pattern pieces are cut on the bias.

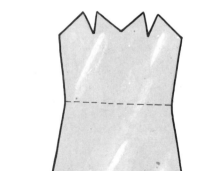

3 Mark a line $2\frac{1}{2}$in (6.5cm) long up center front and center back, starting from the lower edge, with a row of basting. Mark the waistline with basting.

4 Cut a piece of lace to match the top of the back bodice, a piece to match each side of the front and a piece for the V-neck center front. Pin, baste and stitch lace in place following the Technique tip on page 108. Miter the lace and finish it at center front.

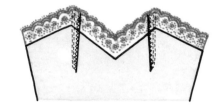

5 Pin, baste and stitch bust darts, continuing dart through lace. Work a second row of stitching $\frac{1}{8}$in (3mm) from first. Trim excess fabric close to second line of stitches and finish raw edges with zig-zag stitch or overcasting. Note that the seam allowance on the darts is only $\frac{1}{4}$in (6mm.)

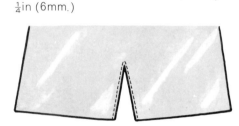

6 Staystitch close to line marked at center front and center back for crotch as shown. Slash up marked line.
7 Cut four pieces of lace to fit around lower edges of legs. Pin, baste and stitch in place following Technique tip.
8 Open out slash on center front and pin, baste and stitch one pointed end of front gusset in place, right sides together. Taper seam allowance on main part to a minimum at the point of the slash. Press seam allowance toward gusset and trim.

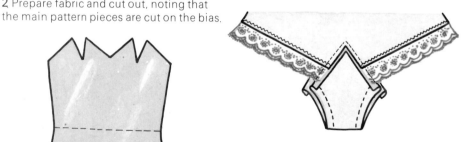

9 Turn under and press seam allowance along free edge of front gusset. Fold back along foldline, right sides together. Pin, baste and stitch side edges together, raw edges matching. Turn gusset right side out and slip stitch turned-under edge of gusset to line of stitching.
10 Repeat steps 8 and 9 to attach back gusset to center back slit.
11 Sew buttons to front gusset, positioning them $\frac{5}{8}$in (1.5cm) from edges and spacing them evenly. Work button loops on fold of back gusset.

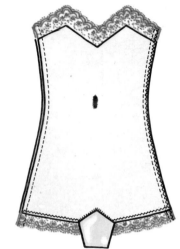

12 Work a $\frac{1}{2}$in (1.3cm) buttonhole at center front waistline.

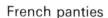

13 With right sides together and raw edges matching, pin, baste and stitch side seams. Add a second line of stitching $\frac{1}{4}$in (6mm) outside the first. Trim away excess fabric and finish with zig-zag stitches or overcasting.
14 Place wide ribbon for casing on wrong side of teddy, positioning it over the middle of the waistline with ends at one side seam. Trim to fit waistline, allowing $\frac{1}{2}$in (1.3cm) at each end for finishing. Join ends to form a ring, finishing the ends as you join them. Stitch casing in place.
15 Cut two pieces of narrow satin ribbon approximately 20in (50cm) long for shoulder straps. Pin in place, try for fit and sew in place securely. Thread remaining ribbon through waist casing.

French panties

Materials

$\frac{5}{8}$yd (.5m) of 54in (140cm)-wide fabric or $1\frac{1}{4}$yd (1.1m) of 36in (90cm)-wide fabric
$1\frac{3}{4}$yd (1.5m) of $2\frac{1}{2}$in (6cm)-wide lace
Waist length plus 1in (2.5cm) of $\frac{1}{4}$in (6mm)-wide elastic
Matching thread
Yardstick; flexible curve; paper for pattern

1 Draw the pattern pieces, making the waist cutting line $\frac{5}{8}$in (1.5cm) above marked waistline.
2 Prepare the fabric and cut out, noting that the main pattern pieces are cut on the bias.
3 Follow steps 6 and 7 of the directions for the teddy to prepare the legs and attach lace.

Terry Evans

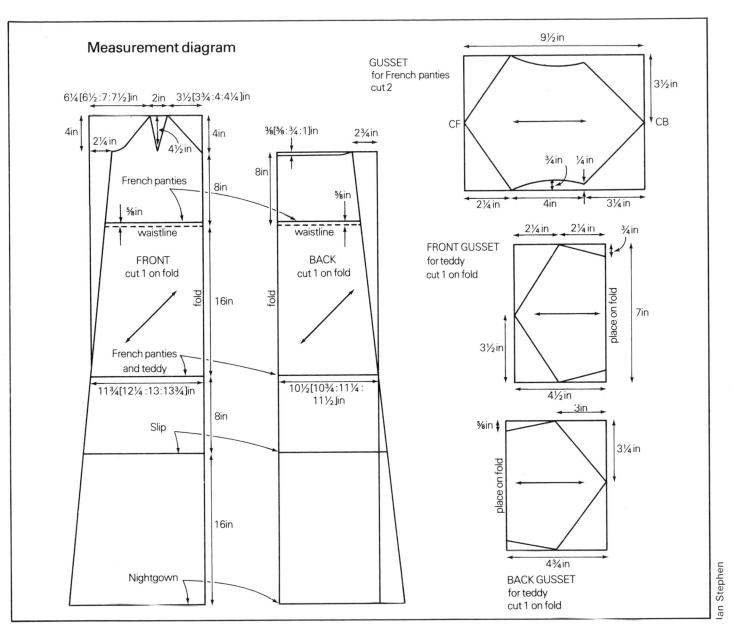

Measurement diagram

GUSSET
for French panties
cut 2

9½in

3½in

CF · · · · · CB

¾in ¼in

2¼in 4in 3¼in

6¼[6½:7:7½]in 2in 3½[3¾:4:4¼]in

4in

2¼ in 4½ in

French panties

⅝in

waistline

FRONT
cut 1 on fold

fold

16in

French panties
and teddy

11¾[12¼:13:13¾]in

Slip

8in

Nightgown

16in

⅜[⅝:¾:1]in 2¾in

8in

⅝in

waistline

BACK
cut 1 on fold

fold

16in

10½[10¾:11¼:11½]in

8in

FRONT GUSSET
for teddy
cut 1 on fold

2¼in 2¼in ¾in

3½ in

place on fold 7in

4½in

BACK GUSSET
for teddy
cut 1 on fold

3in

⅝in

place on fold

3¼ in

4¾in

Ian Stephen

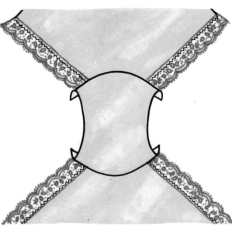

4 Open out slashes on center front and center back and pin, baste and stitch gusset section in place. Turn under ⅝in (1.5cm) along side edges of gusset and clip into curves.
5 Turn under ⅝in (1.5cm) all around gusset lining and clip as necessary.

6 Pin gusset lining in place and slip stitch by hand.
7 Stitch side seams as for teddy.

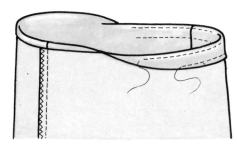

8 Turn under 2in (5cm) and then a further ⅝in (1.5cm) around waist edge. Pin and baste in place. Stitch in place with two rows of stitching, each ⅛in (3mm) from folded edges, leaving an opening for elastic. Thread elastic through, pinning temporarily. Try for fit, then sew ends of elastic securely. Slip stitch opening to close.

Slip

Materials

2yd (1.7m) of 45in (115cm)-wide fabric
3¾yd (3.4m) of lace for bodice, hem and side opening
1¼yd (1m) of ⅜in (1cm)-wide satin ribbon for shoulder straps
Waist length plus 1in (2.5cm) of ¼in (6mm)-wide elastic
1¼yd (1m) of ¾in (2cm)-wide ribbon for casing
Matching thread, flexible curve, yardstick, paper for pattern

1 Follow steps 1–5 of teddy to cut out, apply lace around bodice and stitch darts.
2 Cut two lengths of lace to fit around lower edge of slip, leaving a free length of lace to miter front and back corners at left-hand side. Cut two pieces 12in (30cm) long for side slits.

Applying lace to the edge of a garment

Lace is available in a variety of styles and widths. For this set of lingerie we have used nylon lace in several different widths. The method is adaptable for any width, since the fabric is trimmed after the lace has been applied. The method is really only suitable if you have a machine that does zig-zag stitch. Choose a sewing thread that matches the lace rather than the fabric.

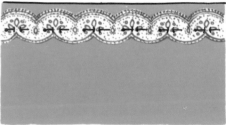

Pin and baste the lace to the right side of the fabric so that the outer edge of the lace matches the raw edge of the fabric. If using a deeply scalloped lace, position it so that the raw edge is half way above the scallops as shown.

Stitch the lace in position, following the inner edge of the lace (which may be shaped or straight). Add a second line of stitching $\frac{1}{8}$in (3mm) away from the first. This will hold the lace firmly in place.

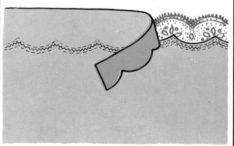

Set the sewing machine to satin stitch or a very short zig-zag and stitch between the first two rows.
Trim away the excess fabric from behind the lace.
If you are using eyelet lace, turn under the raw edge of the lace and then stitch in place in the same way.

---

3 Stitch side seams as described for teddy in step 13. The right-hand side seam ends about 10in (25cm) above the hem. Trim off seam allowance down each side of slit.

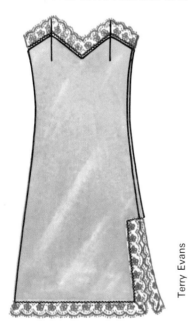

Terry Evans

4 Stitch the pieces of lace in place, mitering corners, following the Technique tip.
5 Pin casing ribbon over waistline, positioning ends of casing at side seam,

centering ribbon over waistline. Baste and stitch in place, leaving an opening for waist elastic.
6 Thread elastic through casing and pin temporarily. Pin shoulder straps in place. Try for fit. Sew waist elastic and shoulder straps firmly in place.

Nightgown

Materials

2yd (1.9m) of 45in (115cm)-wide fabric
5yd (4.6m) of lace for bodice, hem and side openings
3½yd (3m) of ⅜in (1cm)-wide satin ribbon
1¼yd (1.1m) of ⅜in (1cm)-wide ribbon for casing
Matching thread, yardstick, flexible curve, paper for pattern

1 Follow steps 1–5 of teddy. You will need to piece the fabric, using an unwanted corner to achieve the full width. Position seamline across lower corners.
2 Follow steps 2–4 of slip to apply lace and stitch side seams, leaving a 30in (75cm) slit up the right-hand side seam.
3 Make a buttonhole in the center front and complete waist casings as described for teddy, step 14.
4 Complete nightgown as described for teddy, step 15.

SEWING

Two stunning jackets in soft luxurious mohair: one for mother, one for daughter. Both are made from the same basic shape and lined with a coordinated print fabric.

Double act

Belinda

Woman's jacket

Measurements
To fit sizes 10/12.
Finished length: 24½in (62cm).

Suggested fabrics
For jacket: mohair, acrylic fleece.
For lining: printed cotton, printed wool.

Materials
1⅝yd (1.4m) of 59in (150cm)-wide
  mohair
1⅝yd (1.4m) of 59in (150cm)-wide
  lining
Matching thread; paper for pattern
Yardstick; pencil

1 Since it is difficult to mark directly on mohair, make a paper pattern for the main shape, following the diagram.
2 From mohair cut out the back and front piece. Also cut two pockets and six ties from the measurements given.
From lining cut out main pattern piece and six ties. ⅝in (1.5cm) seam allowances have been included and 1¼in (3cm) hems.

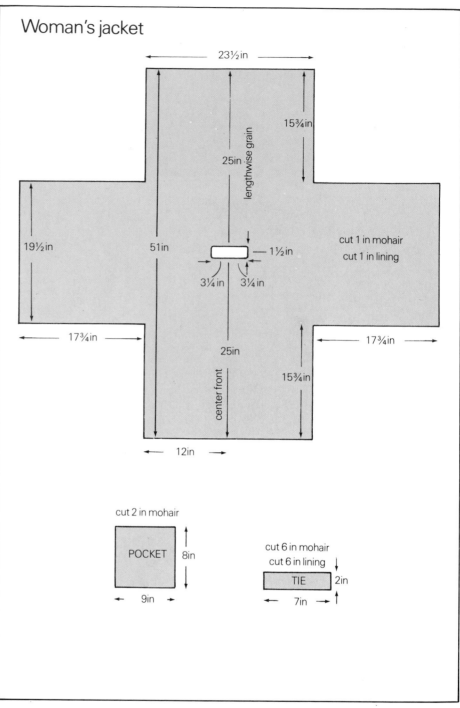

Woman's jacket

23½in

15¾in

lengthwise grain

25in

19½in

51in

1½in

cut 1 in mohair
cut 1 in lining

3¼in   3¼in

17¾in

25in

17¾in

center front

15¾in

12in

cut 2 in mohair

POCKET   8in

9in

cut 6 in mohair
cut 6 in lining

TIE   2in

7in

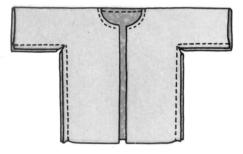

3 Staystitch around the neck of the mohair piece to prevent stretching. Fold the mohair section along shoulder line and stitch underarm and side seams. Clip corners and overcast neatly to prevent raveling. Press seams open.
With right sides together and raw edges even, stitch lining underarm and side seam. Clip corners, finish and press.

4 Fringe the top 1½in (4cm) of both mohair pocket pieces. Turn in and baste ⅜in (1cm) hems around remaining edges.

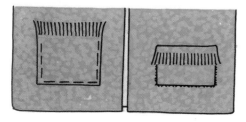

5 Position each mohair pocket on right

side of jacket, 2in (5cm) from center front and 3½in (9cm) from bottom edge. Slip stitch in place, turning over tops.

6 With right sides together, pin and baste each mohair tie to corresponding lining tie. Stitch all around, leaving an opening in one side. Turn right side out and slip stitch opening. Press.
7 Turn up hem on mohair jacket and herringbone stitch. Turn up hem on lining and machine-stitch.

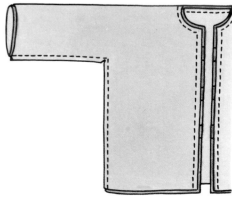

8 With right sides together, slip lining over mohair jacket. Position ties so that

they are sandwiched between mohair and lining, with mohair facing mohair and lining to lining. Pin, baste and stitch neck and center front seams, catching in ties. Turn right side out, slipping lining inside jacket.

9 Turn up mohair and lining sleeve hems for ⅝in (1.5cm) and slip stitch together.

Child's jacket

Measurements
To fit ages 4 to 7.
Finished length: 18½in (47cm).

Materials
1⅛yd (1m) of 48in (122cm)-wide mohair
1⅛yd (1m) of 48in (122cm)-wide lining
Matching thread; paper for pattern
Yardstick; pencil, flexible curve

1 Make pattern, following appropriate measurement diagram. Make pattern for hood

2 Cut out two hood pieces in mohair and two hood pieces in lining fabric.

3 Make jacket, following steps 3 to 9 of directions for mother's jacket, but do not stitch mohair and lining together around neck edge to allow for hood.

4 Stitch mohair hood pieces together down center back seam. With right sides together, stitch lining hood pieces together. Clip curves and press seams.

5 With right sides together, slip mohair hood into lining hood and stitch around front edge. Turn right side out and press.

6 Make a tailor's tack along unstitched edge of hood 3¼in (8cm) from front edge on each side as shown. Notch seam

allowance at these points, overcasting mohair to prevent raveling.

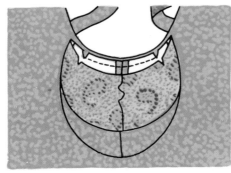

7 Matching center back of hood with center back of jacket and with mohair sides facing, pin and baste hood to jacket. Ease hood onto jacket, as far as tailor's tacks, which should correspond to jacket center fronts. Stitch, leaving hood lining free.

8 Turn lining back 3¼in (8cm). Turn under seam allowances still open and slip stitch them together, catching edges along neck edge seam.
Turn in seam allowance around neck edge of lining hood and slip stitch in place. Catch-stitch turned-back edge to center seam.

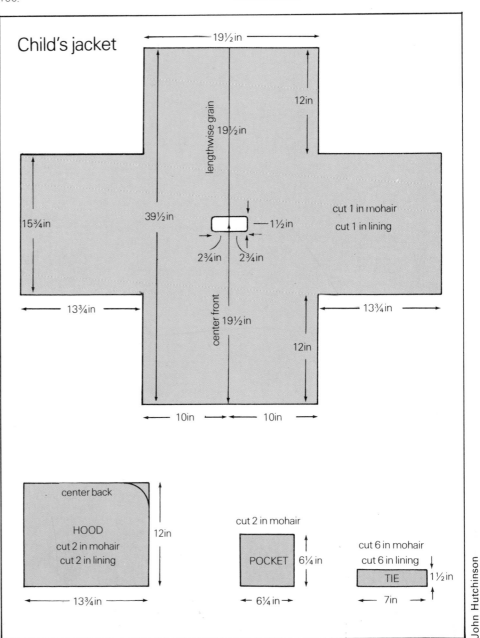

Child's jacket

19½in
12in
lengthwise grain
19½in
39½in
15¾in
cut 1 in mohair
cut 1 in lining
1½in
2¾in 2¾in
13¾in
center front
19½in
13¾in
12in
10in 10in

center back
HOOD
cut 2 in mohair
cut 2 in lining
12in
13¾in

cut 2 in mohair
POCKET
6¼in
6¼in

cut 6 in mohair
cut 6 in lining
TIE
1½in
7in

Technique tip

Working with mohair

Mohair tends to ravel, so overcast any cut edges.

Self-fringed edges are easy to make. Simply pull away the horizontal threads to make the depth of fringe required. Make pattern markings with tailor's tacks, as chalk will not mark the fabric. Hand-sewing is easier than machine stitching and it pulls the fabric less. Use herring-bone stitch for hems.

When machine-stitching is needed for strength, as in the underarm seams of the jackets shown, use a longer machine stitch than normal. Practice on a scrap of spare fabric, adjusting the presser foot if necessary.

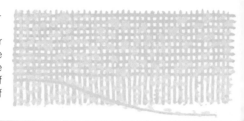

Simon Butcher

Needlework

Co-ordinating prints

This beautiful patchwork bedspread is made from six harmonizing fabrics using triangles, rectangles and squares. It is constructed by the traditional block method and machine-stitched.

Belinda

Finished size

About 98×86in (250×220cm). Suitable for a double bed.
A seam allowance of $\frac{3}{8}$in (1cm) has been included throughout.

Materials

45in (115cm)-wide printed fabrics
2$\frac{3}{4}$yd (2.5m) of fabric A
2$\frac{1}{4}$yd (2m) of fabric B
1$\frac{1}{8}$yd (1m) of fabric C
1$\frac{1}{8}$yd (1m) of fabric D
3$\frac{3}{8}$yd (3m) of fabric E
$\frac{3}{4}$yd (.6m) of fabric F
5$\frac{1}{2}$yd (5.1m) of 45in (115cm)-wide fabric for lining
Matching thread; soft pencil
Thin cardboard
Ruler and right triangle

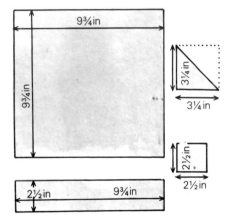

1 Using the triangle and ruler, draw the patchwork templates on cardboard, following the measurements above. Cut out each template.
2 Using a soft pencil and working on the wrong side of the fabric, draw around each template on the appropriate fabric to give the correct number of patches (see below). When marking, place the templates on the straight grain of the fabric and leave a $\frac{3}{8}$in (1cm) margin around each one. Include this when cutting out patches.
3 From fabric A cut out 16 large squares. Cut out 144 triangles.
4 From fabric B cut out 12 large squares. Cut out 108 triangles.
5 From fabric C cut out 144 triangles.
6 From fabric D cut out 108 triangles.
7 From fabric E cut out 127 border rectangles.
8 From fabric F cut out 72 small border squares.

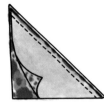

9 Join two triangles—one of fabric A and one of C—to form a square, placing them

together with right sides facing and edges matching. Pin, baste and stitch along the diagonal edge.
10 Repeat step 9 to join all the triangles in fabrics A and C into squares.
11 Repeat step 9 to make squares in the same way using triangles of fabrics B and D. Take care in joining the triangles that the corners meet exactly.

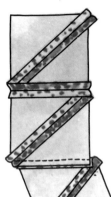

12 Join three of the A/C squares to form a strip. Place two squares together with right sides facing and edges matching and with the diagonal seams running from top right to bottom left. Pin, baste and stitch together.
Repeat to stitch third square to the previous two.
13 Repeat step 12 to make two more strips of A/C triangles.

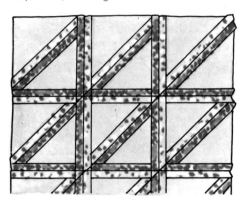

14 Join these three strips together to form one large square. Place two strips together with right sides facing and long edges matching. Make sure that the crosswise seams match and that the diagonal seams are all running in the same direction—from top right to bottom left. Pin, baste and stitch the long edges together. Repeat to stitch third strip to the other two strips.
15 Repeat steps 12 to 14 to make 15 more large patchwork squares of A/C triangles.
16 Repeat steps 12 to 14 to make 12 large squares of B/D triangles.
17 Place one border rectangle along top edge of one triangle patchwork square. Place them together with right sides facing and edges matching. Pin, baste and stitch.

18 Repeat step 17 to join a border rectangle to the top edge of each triangle patchwork square in the same way.
19 Repeat step 17 to join one border rectangle to one side of each large square of fabrics A and B.

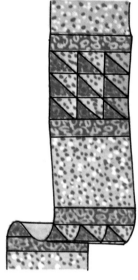

20 Join four A/C triangle patchwork squares to four plain large squares of fabric A, alternating the large squares and positioning them so that the border rectangles are always between the squares. Begin by joining two bordered squares in this order: fabric A square, border, patchwork square, border. Place them together with right sides facing and edges matching. Pin, baste and stitch along the first border-patchwork edge. Repeat until there are eight squares in each strip.
21 Pin, baste and stitch a border rectangle to the free edge of the first square.

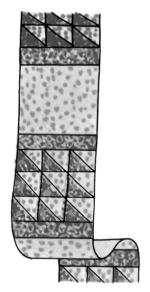

22 Repeat steps 20 and 21 using patchwork squares of B/D triangles and plain squares of fabric B, joining them with a border between each, as before, but beginning with a patchwork square.

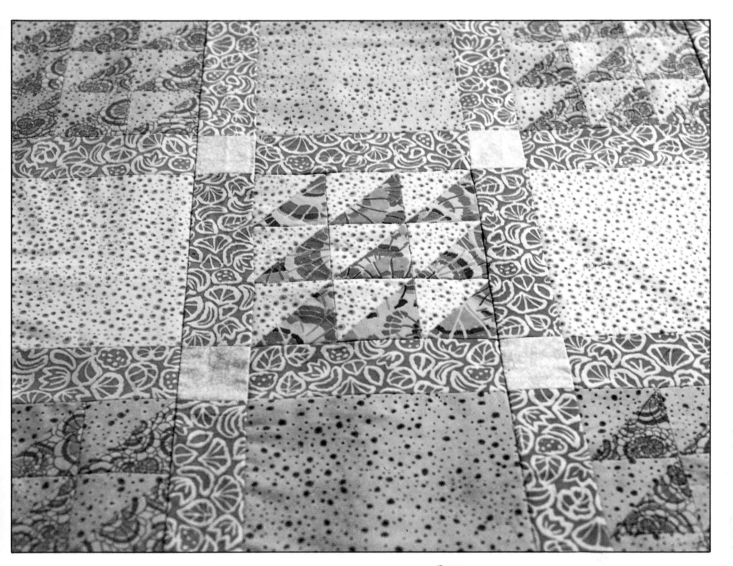

23 Repeat steps 20 to 22 to make five more patchwork strips in the same way as the first.

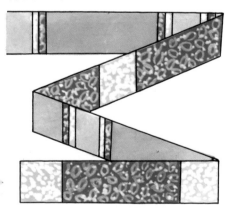

24 Join eight border rectangles to nine small border squares to form a strip, alternating the two shapes and placing a border square at each end. Place the first square on the first rectangle with right sides together and edges matching. Pin, baste and stitch together. Repeat to complete the strip.
25 Repeat step 24 and make seven more strips in the same way.

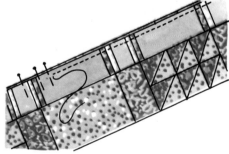

26 With right sides facing, join right-hand edge of one rectangle-square strip to left-hand edge of a wide A and C fabric strip so that there is a large plain square at the top. Place the strips together with right sides facing and edges matching. Pin, baste and stitch. Press the seams open.
27 Repeat step 26 to make six more double strips in the same way, stitching a border strip to the left-hand side of each wide strip. Make sure that all seams meet exactly and that when stitched together the large plain squares will alternate with the triangle patchwork squares vertically as well as horizontally across the bedspread.

28 Join the resulting double strips together, alternating A/C fabric strips with B/D strips so that plain and patchwork squares also alternate. Place the first two strips together with right sides facing, edges matching and the border strips separating the two strips of squares. Pin, baste and stitch together. Repeat to join all the strips.
29 Join the remaining border strip to the right-hand edge of the finished patchwork.
30 Cut the lining fabric in half crosswise and join the two halves with a plain seam to make a piece measuring 99 × 90in (252 × 230cm). Press the seam open and finish it.
31 Lay the lining fabric flat with wrong side up. Place the patchwork right side up and centered on the lining fabric. Pin and baste the two layers together.
32 Trim the lining fabric to within $\frac{3}{4}$in (2cm) of the edge of the patchwork.
33 Turn down the edge of the lining fabric $\frac{3}{8}$in (1cm), then fold it over onto the patchwork, mitering the corners neatly. Pin, baste and stitch the hem in place using a zig-zag machine stitch. Alternately, you can slip stitch the hem by hand.

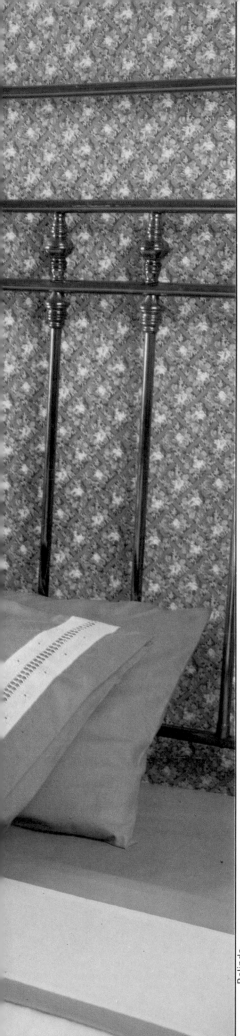

Needlework

Decorative drawn thread work

Bring a touch of individuality to plain bed linens with drawn thread work. Embroider the design on a strip of linen and sew this to the edge of a sheet or pillowcase.

Finished size
Triangular design: 7in (18cm) deep and 21in (54cm) wide; pillowcase design, as width of pillowcase.

Materials
*A sheet in a solid color
A matching pillowcase
Length of white evenweave linen to go across sheet plus ¾in (2cm)
4 skeins of stranded embroidery floss
Matching sewing thread; ruler*

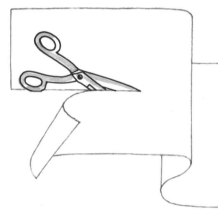

1 Cut a strip of linen 12in (31cm) × width of sheet plus ¾in (2cm).

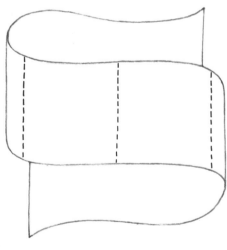

2 Mark the center of the strip widthwise with a line of basting. Add two more lines of basting, 18in (46cm) to each side of the center line.

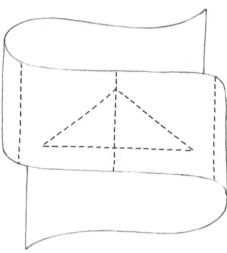

3 Inside this center panel measure and mark a triangle with basting: measure 2¼in (6cm) down the center line. Measure down a further 7in (18cm); at this point mark a horizontal line 10½in (27cm) to each side of center line. Connect the ends to upper point.
4 This marked triangle is filled with drawn thread work. Use 6 strands of embroidery floss throughout and work downward.

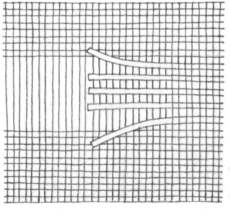

Terry Evans

5 Before working each row, first withdraw the threads from the fabric, carefully cutting them individually at the center and then easing them out toward the basted line at the side of the triangle. Darn loose ends in on wrong side. Work the embroidery downward from the base of the triangle.

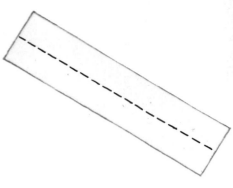

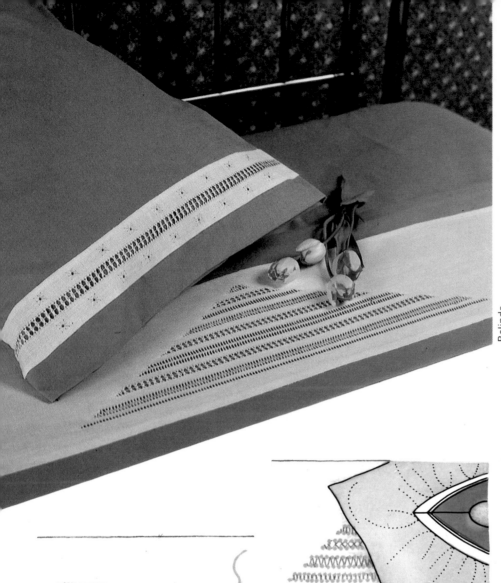

Belinda

19 Mark the center of the strip lengthwise with basting stitches.
20 Work a line of interlaced hemstitch down this marked center line.
21 Work star eyelets on each side of the center row, placing the centers of the eyelets ⅝in (1.5cm) from the center line and spacing them 1¾in (4.5cm) apart.
22 Turn under ⅜in (1cm) on both long edges; pin and baste.
23 Unpick the side seams of the pillowcase for 6¼in (16cm) alongside the hem.

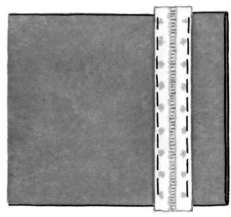

24 Place the strip on the right side of the pillowcase, with one long edge against hem; pin and baste it in place.

25 Push the short edges of strip into the openings in the seams. Pin, baste and stitch the pillowcase seams again, catching in short edges of strip.
26 Neatly hand-hem the long edges of the strip to the pillowcase.

6 Starting at the base of the triangle, work a row of ladder hemstitch.
7 Work a row of zig-zag hemstitch ¼in (5mm) below the first row.
8 Work a row of interlaced hemstitch ⅜in (1cm) below the zig-zag hemstitch.
9 Work 2 rows of ladder hemstitch, close together, ⅜in (1cm) below the previous row.
10 Work a row of interlaced hemstitch ⅜in (1cm) below the ladder hemstitch.
11 Work a row of zig-zag hemstitch ⅜in (1cm) below the interlaced hemstitch.
12 Work a row of ladder hemstitch ⅜in (1cm) below the previous row.
13 Work a row of interlaced hemstitch ¼in (5mm) below the ladder hemstitch.
14 To finish the top of the triangle work a row of zig-zag hemstitch ⅜in (1cm) below the previous row.

15 When the embroidery is complete, press it well on the wrong side, using a steam iron or a dry iron over a damp cloth.
16 Turn under ⅜in (1cm) along all edges of the fabric strip, mitering the corners neatly. Pin and baste.

17 Place the strip, right side up, on the top edge of the sheet, with the long edge against the stitching on the hem. Pin and baste it in place. Hand-hem.
18 From remaining linen cut a strip 6½in (17cm) wide × width of the pillowcase plus ¾in (2cm).

Drawn thread work stitches

Ladder hemstitch

This stitch consists of two rows of hemstitch, one row worked on each side of a space from which threads have been withdrawn.

Withdraw the appropriate number of threads—for this project, to a depth of $\frac{1}{4}$ in (5mm). Bring the working thread out 2 fabric threads down from the drawn thread area and through the fabric at the right-hand side. Pass the needle behind 4 vertical threads, then take the needle behind the same 4 threads and bring it out 2 threads down as before, in readiness for the next stitch.

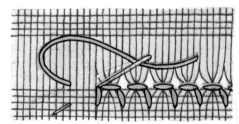

Repeat along the opposite edge.

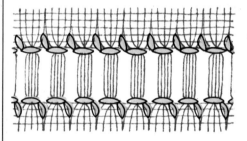

Zig-zag hemstitch

This is another variation of hemstitch. Begin by working a row of hemstitch over an even number of threads. Then work hemstitch along the opposite edge, splitting up the groups of threads already formed. Each stitch is worked over half the threads from one group and half from the next. A half group starts and ends the second row of embroidery. For this project withdraw threads to a depth of $\frac{5}{8}$ in (1.5cm).

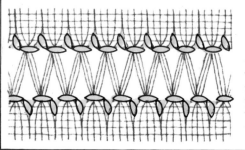

Interlaced hemstitch

Work ladder hemstitch first. Then fasten a long thread at the right-hand side at the middle of the vertical threads. Pass the working threads across the front of two groups of threads, then from left to right under the second group. Twist the second group over the first by inserting the needle under the first group from right to left.

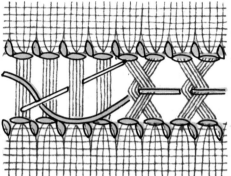

Pull the thread through so that it is correctly positioned at the center of the twisted groups.
For this project withdraw threads to a depth of $\frac{1}{2}$ in (1.3cm).

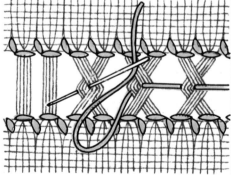

Star eyelet

This eyelet consists of 8 stitches worked over a square of fabric, 8 threads each way.
Work all the stitches from the same central hole. Pull each thread gently outward to open the center hole.

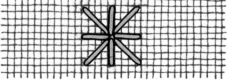

Homemaker

Simple sofa

Our easy-to-make sofa is constructed from two blocks of solid foam and polystyrene beads and is covered with attractive, durable corduroy.

Key for 60in (152cm)-wide fabric

A Seat
B Seat side ends
C Seat sides
D Arm/back ends
E Backs
F Back base
G Arms
H Arm bases

Key for 45in (115cm)-wide fabric

D Arm/back ends
E Backs
F Back base
G Arms
H Arm bases

Finished size

75×27in (190×69cm), 26in (66cm) high. A seam allowance of ¾in (2cm) is included.

Materials

Two pieces of foam 75×27in (190×69cm), 7½in (19cm) thick
10yd (9.2m) of 60in (152cm)-wide heavyweight corduroy
Polystyrene beads for arms and back
5⅝yd (4.9m) of 45in (115cm)-wide unbleached muslin
¾yd (.7m) of 36in (90cm)-wide iron-on interfacing
Two pieces of stiff cardboard 16×10 in (41×25cm) for arm bases
Piece of stiff cardboard 74½×10in (189×25cm) for back base
6½yd (6m) of ⅝in (1.5cm) wide heavy-duty snap fastening tape
Matching thread; paper for pattern

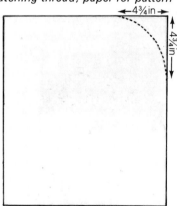

1 Make a paper pattern for the arm/back ends. On a piece of paper draw a rectangle 12½×11¾in (32×30cm). Mark a point 4¾in (12cm) in from one corner on both top and sides. Draw a curve from point to point. Cut along the marked curve. Fold the pattern in half lengthwise; mark and round off the opposite corner in the same way.
2 Cut out all the corduroy pieces, following the cutting layout.
3 Use the pattern to cut six arm/back ends from interfacing. Place them shiny side down on wrong side of corduroy end pieces. Iron in place.

4 Place two seat side pieces together with right sides facing and edges matching. Pin, baste and stitch one short edge.
5 Repeat step 4 with two more seat side pieces.

6 Position one seat side end piece between the two joined side pieces with right sides together and short edges matching. Pin, baste and stitch.
7 Repeat step 6 with other side end piece, so that all the side pieces now form a ring.

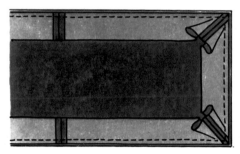

8 Place the complete side piece on one main seat piece with right sides facing and the side end pieces at the short ends of the main piece. Check that the four end seams match the corners exactly. The pile on the side piece should run upward. Pin, baste and stitch the side and main pieces together around all four edges.
9 Repeat step 8 to pin and baste the other main seat piece to the opposite edge of side piece in the same way, to complete the base. Stitch together all around, leaving open one short edge and 20in (50cm) along both adjacent sides.
10 Trim seams and turn seat cover right side out. Insert one piece of foam into the cover. Pin opening edges together to close them temporarily.
11 Repeat steps 4 to 10 to make and fill other seat cover.

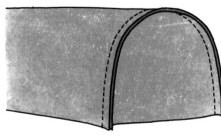

12 Place the long edge of one rectangular arm piece on the curved edge of one arm end, with right sides together. Pin and baste the two edges together, easing the rectangular piece evenly around the curve. Stitch.
13 Repeat step 12 to join another arm end to the free edge of the arm piece.

14 Make a line of basting stitches on both long edges of one arm base, 1½in (4cm) in from the edges, starting and finishing 1½in (4cm) from the ends.
15 Cut two pieces of fastening tape the same measurement as basted lines.

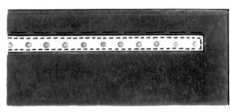

16 Place the top half of each length of fastening tape on arm base with outer edges meeting the basted lines; turn ends under neatly. Pin, baste and stitch the fastening tape in place along all four edges of each piece. Put the matching lengths of tape aside; they will be stitched to one of the seat covers.

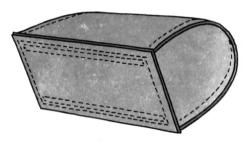

17 Place arm base on arm piece with right sides together. Pin, baste and stitch them together, leaving the seam open at base of one end. Trim seams, trimming the interfacing close to the seamline; clip curves. Turn arm right side out.
18 Cut out arm and back pieces from muslin, following the cutting layout.
19 Repeat steps 12, 13 and 17 to assemble a muslin lining arm in the same way, again leaving open the base seam at one end. Trim seams, clip curves and turn lining arm right side out.
20 Place the muslin arm inside corduroy arm with right side of muslin to wrong side of corduroy and seams matching.
21 Place one of the cardboard bases inside the muslin arm. Stuff the muslin

arm firmly with beads. Turn in the opening edges on muslin arm and slip stitch them firmly together. Repeat on corduroy arm.
22 Repeat steps 12 to 17 and 19 to 21 to make another arm piece. Before joining corduroy end pieces to main arm piece, place completed arm with slip stitched end to a wall. The side with the pile running upward will face inward on the sofa. Assemble the second arm with pile running in the opposite direction and opening at the back, as on first arm.

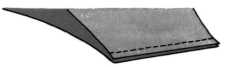

23 Place the corduroy back pieces together with right sides facing and edges matching. Pin, baste and stitch one short edge for center seam.
24 Repeat step 23 with the muslin back pieces.
25 Assemble the back in the same way as the arms, steps 12 to 17 and steps 19 to 21.
26 Position the back and arms on top of one seat cover with pile running upward on inner arms and back and outer edges aligned. Mark the positions of the fastening tape on the seat cover.

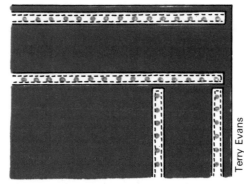

Terry Evans

27 Remove the piece of foam from the cover. Position the matching halves of each length of fastening tape on the seat cover at the sides and back edge, matching the marks. Pin, baste and stitch each piece in place on all four edges.
28 Replace the cover on the piece of foam. Turn in the opening edges on the cover. Slip stitch the opening edges firmly together.
29 Slip stitch the opening edges together on the other seat cover.
30 Place the upper seat on top of the other one, matching all edges. Fasten the back and the arms to the seat with the fastening tape.

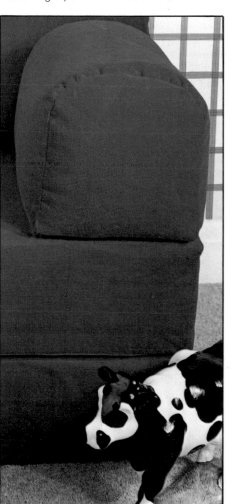

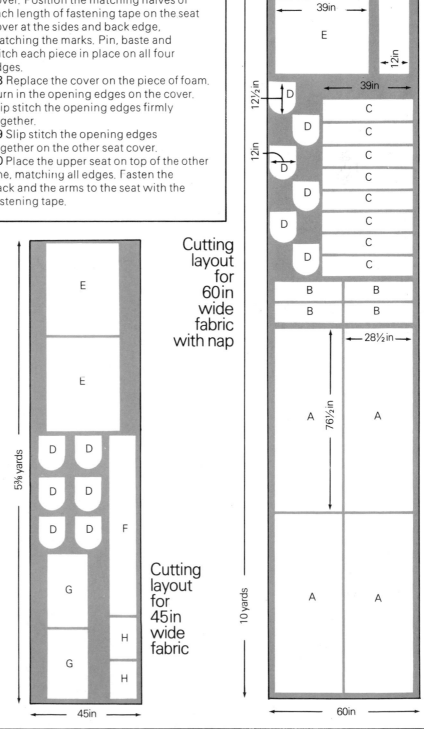

Cutting layout for 60in wide fabric with nap

Cutting layout for 45in wide fabric

John Hutchinson

123

Homemaker

Playful puppets

Jungle adventures are fun to make up and enact with these feline glove puppets.

Finished size
Puppets are about 12½in (32cm) tall.

Tiger

Materials
*2 pieces of orange felt and 1 of
   dark brown felt, each 12×9in
   (30×23cm)*
*Scraps of white, black, green and
   pink felt*
Black and white pearl cotton
Matching thread
Tracing paper; pinking shears
Dressmaker's carbon paper
*½yd (.5m) of ⅜in (1cm)-wide green
   satin ribbon*

1 Trace the pattern pieces for the
tiger on pages 126-127.
2 Mark the pattern pieces on one side of
the appropriate felt, the number of times
stated. Cut out. Cut tongue from pink
felt. Use pinking shears for the inner ears,
cheeks and face and body stripes.
3 Stitch the features to the face on the
front body piece. Place the features on
the face in the order given here: first
position the stripes on the face; pin,
baste and stitch close to long edges.

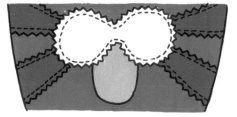

4 Position the tongue on the face, then
place the cheeks over the top of the
tongue. Pin, baste and stitch the cheeks
in place, stitching close to the edge and
catching in the top of the tongue.
5 Center the nose over the cheeks. Pin,
baste and stitch in place, stitching close
to edge and down center.

6 Sew a highlight on the nose: using
white pearl cotton and straight stitches
work a small circle on the right-hand side.

7 Make an eye: place the outer eye on the
face. Pin, baste and stitch in place,
stitching close to the edge.

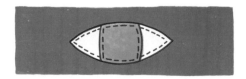

8 Pin, baste and stitch the iris to the
center of the outer eye, again stitching
close to the edge.

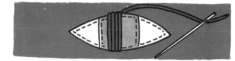

9 Work a few straight stitches in black
pearl cotton over the center of the iris
for the pupil.
10 Repeat steps 7 to 9 to make the other
eye in the same way.

11 Work a single French knot in white
pearl cotton on the right-hand side of
each pupil to give the eyes sparkle.
12 Work French knots in black pearl
cotton all over both the cheeks.

13 To make the front ear, center one
inner ear on one outer ear. Pin, baste and
stitch in place, stitching close to the edge
as shown.

14 Place one front ear right side down,
on one plain back ear. Pin, baste and
stitch around ears, taking ¼in (5mm)
seam allowances and leaving straight
bottom edges open. Trim seam and turn
ear right side out.
15 Repeat steps 13 and 14 to make the
other ear in the same way.

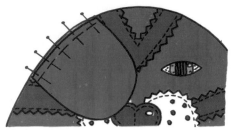

16 Place ears on face, with right sides
together, at positions marked. Match raw
edges so that ears point inward. Pin and
baste ears in place.

17 Position paw pads on one paw,
placing one foot pad and three toe pads
as shown. Pin, baste and slip stitch pads
in place, stitching close to the edges.
18 Repeat step 17 to sew pads to other
paw in the same way.

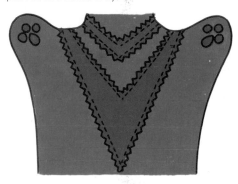

19 Position body stripes on front body,
with the smaller stripe above the larger
one. Pin, baste and stitch stripes in place,
stitching close to both long edges.
20 Place back body on front body with
right sides together. Pin, baste and stitch
all around, taking a ¼in (5mm) seam
allowance and catching in ears. Leave
straight bottom edges open.
21 Trim seam and turn tiger puppet right
side out. Press puppet gently into shape.

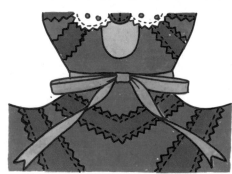

Terry Evans

22 Tie the green ribbon around the tiger's
neck and into a bow. Snip the ribbon ends
into "V"s to finish them.

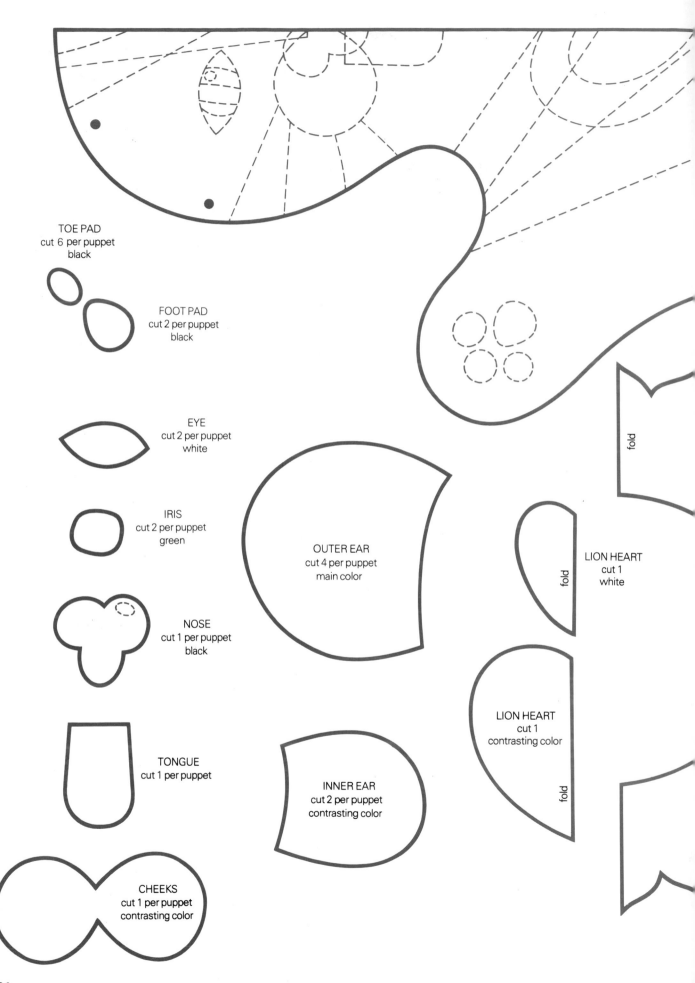

TOE PAD
cut 6 per puppet
black

FOOT PAD
cut 2 per puppet
black

EYE
cut 2 per puppet
white

IRIS
cut 2 per puppet
green

NOSE
cut 1 per puppet
black

OUTER EAR
cut 4 per puppet
main color

fold

LION HEART
cut 1
white

fold

LION HEART
cut 1
contrasting color

TONGUE
cut 1 per puppet

INNER EAR
cut 2 per puppet
contrasting color

fold

CHEEKS
cut 1 per puppet
contrasting color

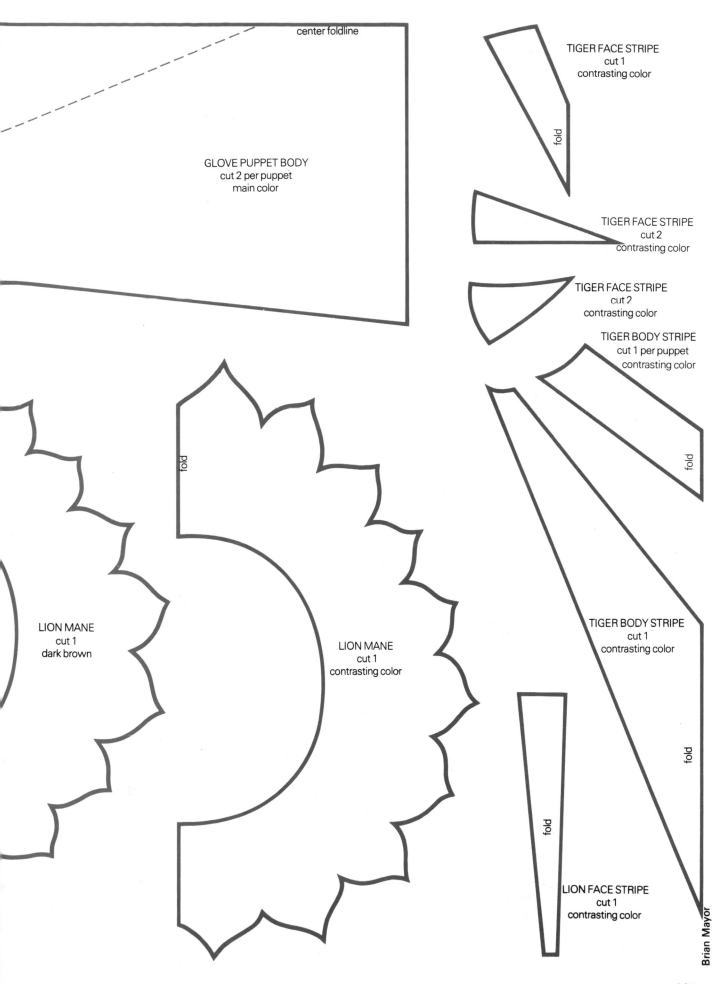

center foldline

GLOVE PUPPET BODY
cut 2 per puppet
main color

TIGER FACE STRIPE
cut 1
contrasting color

fold

TIGER FACE STRIPE
cut 2
contrasting color

TIGER FACE STRIPE
cut 2
contrasting color

TIGER BODY STRIPE
cut 1 per puppet
contrasting color

fold

fold

LION MANE
cut 1
dark brown

LION MANE
cut 1
contrasting color

TIGER BODY STRIPE
cut 1
contrasting color

fold

fold

LION FACE STRIPE
cut 1
contrasting color

Brian Mayor

127

Lion

Materials

*Two pieces of gold felt, each
    12 × 9in (30 × 23cm)*
*One piece of rust felt and one of
    dark brown felt, each 12 × 9in
    (30 × 23cm)*
*Scraps of green, black, white and
    red felt*
Black and white pearl cotton
Matching thread
Tracing paper; pinking shears
Dressmaker's carbon paper
*½yd (.5m) of ⅜in (1cm)-wide blue
    satin ribbon*

1 Trace the pattern pieces for the lion given on pages 126-127.
2 Mark the pattern pieces on one side of the appropriate felt, the number of times stated. Cut out. Cut tongue from red felt. Use pinking shears for the inner ears, cheeks, face stripe and hearts.
3 Stitch the features to the face on the front body piece. Place the features on the face in the order given here: first position the tongue on the face with the cheeks over the tongue top. Pin, baste and stitch the cheeks in place, stitching close to the edge and catching in the top of the tongue.
4 Center the face stripe on the top of the face with the widest end at the top. Pin, baste and stitch in place, stitching close to both long edges.
5 Position the nose over the cheeks and stripe. Pin, baste and stitch it in place, stitching close to edge and down center.
6 Sew a highlight on the lion's nose as for the tiger, step 6.
7 Make eyes, as for tiger, steps 7 to 10.
8 Work French knots in white pearl cotton all over both cheeks.
9 Make ears as for the tiger, steps 13 to 16.
10 Position pads on paws on front body piece as for tiger, steps 17 and 18.

11 Center the hearts on the front body piece, with the smaller heart on top of the larger one. Pin, baste and stitch each heart in place, stitching close to the edges.

12 Place the two mane pieces one on top of the other, so that the points appear alternately as shown. Match the inside edges together. Pin and baste them together.

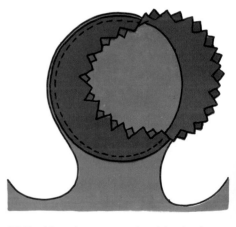

13 Position the mane on back body piece, around the top of the head and across the base of the head in a circular shape with the darker, slightly smaller, mane facing upward and points lying inward. Pin, baste and stitch close to the inner edge to hold the mane in place.
14 Finish the lion as for the tiger, steps 20 to 22, catching in the mane as well as the ears and using blue ribbon for the neck tie.